Creation Fire

A CAFRA ANTHOLOGY OF
CARIBBEAN WOMEN'S POETRY

Edited by RAMABAI ESPINET

Sister Vision
Black Women and Women of Colour Press

CAFRA

ISBN 0-920813-02-X

This book was printed with the generous assistance of **MATCH International Centre** (with support from NGO Division and the Public Participation Programme of CIDA).

Cover Art: "The Tree of Life (The First Strike)" 1983 Batik by Sharon Chacko, Kingston, Jamaica
Cover and Book Design: Stephanie Martin
Typesetting: HINDSight

Printed and Bound in Canada

Canadian Cataloguing in Publication Data Main entry under title:

Creation fire : a CAFRA anthology of Caribbean women's poetry

"This anthology is a CAFRA initiative."
Includes poems in English, Spanish, Dutch and French; those in Spanish, Dutch and French accompanied by translations into English.

ISBN 0-920813-02-X

1.   Caribbean poetry - Women authors.
2.   Caribbean poetry (English).
3.   Caribbean poetry - 20th century. I. Espinet, Ramabai, 1948 - II. CAFRA (Association).

PR2905.6.C74 1990   811   C89-095460-7

Published by :
SISTER VISION
Black Women and Women of Colour Press
P.O. Box 217, Station E
Toronto, Ontario
Canada M6H 4E2

CAFRA
P.O. Bag 442
Tunapuna,
Trinidad and Tobago

The editor and the Publishers would like to thank the following for their kind permission to reprint copyright material in this book:

Sheba Feminist Publishers for 'Lovers'; 'Strangers in a Hostile Landscape'; 'The Knock' and 'The Boat Girl' from Gifts From My Grandmother. 'Shackles', 'Midnight Without Pity' and 'Gifts' by Amryl Johnson from the sequence 'Gorgons' as yet unpublished; Black Scholar Press for "In the Country of Vietnam"; 'An Oakland Apple Tree'; 'Black Woman' and 'Farewell' by Nancy Morejon. Firebrand Books for 'The Land of Look Behind' and 'Love in the Third World' by Michelle Cliff. W.W. Norton & Company, Inc. and Audre Lorde for 'Never to Dream of Spiders'. Audre Lorde for 'Production', 'Coast Market' and 'Judiths Fancy'. Race Today and Jean Breeze for 'Arising'; 'Ordinary Mawning' and 'Dreamer'. Olive Senior for 'The Mother'; 'Colonial Girls School'; 'To the Madwoman in my Yard'. Louise Bennett for 'Dutty Tough' and 'Bans O'Ooman'. Toronto South Asian Review for 'The Vamp's Prize' and 'Diamond' by Mahadai Das. Virago Press for "Praise Song for my Mother" and 'We New World Blacks' by Grace Nichols. Karnak House for 'Omen' and 'Nanny' by Grace Nichols. Karia Press for 'Butterfly Born' by Merle Collins; Nydia Ecury for 'Song for Mother Earth' and 'Old Lady'.

artwork reproduced with permission of:

Stephanie Martin — The Seer
Sandra Leonora — The Artist
Danuta Radzik — The Mother
Danuta Radzik — The Lover
Stephanie Martin — The Exile
Helen Martina — The Mourner
Karen de Souza — The Land
"Emerging" by Stephanie Correia — The Region
Courtesy of Frome Cultural Workers — The Worker
Dawn French — The Guerrilla
Karen de Souza — The Survivor
Zorida Baksh-Rampersad — The Praise Singer

All poems printed with the permission of author.

DEDICATION:
To the courage, heroism and
resistance of the women of the
Caribbean Region

ACKNOWLEDGEMENTS

This book could not have been possible without the faith, goodwill and patience of the poets who so willingly contributed their poems to this anthology. Our first words of thanks go to them.

Special appreciation is due to the support given in CAFRA — ex- members of the Secretariat and others — particularly to Patricia Mohammed, Gemma Tang Nain, Gaietry Pargass, Joan French, Joan Ross-Frankson and Honor Ford-Smith.

The members of the editorial committee (some of them also Secretariat members) — Cathy Shepherd, Margaret Gill, Sonia Cuales, Rawwida Baksh-Soodeen, Rodlyn Douglas, Sharon Lee Wah, Joy Mahabir and Nan Peacocke — gave many long hours in the reading and selection process, and were always available for consultation.

Thanks to all of the CAFRA members in countries throughout the Caribbean who worked to publicize the project and to collect poems, especially Diane Haylock in Belize; Liliane Marchal in Martinique; Nelcia Robinson in St. Vincent and the Grenadines; Chandra Binendijk in Suriname; Indra Chandarpal in Guyana; Gladys Do Rego-Kuster in Curacao and Aruba; Yamila Azize in Puerto Rico, and Catherine Ribas-Hermelo in Cuba.

Thanks to Sharon Chacko for her cover art and for her generosity in making it available to us at an affordable cost, and to all of the other artists for their contributions.

Thanks to all those involved in the translation process and, in particular, to Sonia Cuales, Mariana Valverde and Wendy Waring.

For administrative work well beyond the normal limits, thanks to Joy Mahabir and Tina Johnson.

Thanks to Makeda Silvera and Stephanie Martin of Sister Vision Press, Toronto, for invaluable support and advice throughout the life of this project.

Thanks to the international and regional organizations which supported CAFRA's work during the production of the Anthology, namely UNIFEM, HIVOS, the Dutch Government, the Ford Foundation, WAND, INTER-PARES and CUSO. We would like to record our special thanks to MATCH International Centre for its direct contribution to the publication costs and to the proposed Caribbean and Canadian promotional activities.

To the many more people who have contributed to this work whom we cannot name individually, and to the work of the Women's Movement in the Region, in general, we give our warmest thanks.

PREFACE

The Caribbean Association for Feminist Research and Action, or CAFRA (the acronym by which it is better known) is a membership association of individual feminists, women activists and women's organizations spanning the Dutch, English, French and Spanish-speaking Caribbean and its diaspora.

Its founding in 1985, the year marking the end of the United Nations 'Decade of Women', was one of the signs that the Caribbean women's movement had come of age. In fact, its launching followed on the heels of the Women and Development Unit's (WAND) 'Caribbean Celebration' to mark the end of the decade. However, the philosophical framework shaped by the forty women from across the region who launched the association was radically different from accepted thinking and practice on Women and Development, promulgated by many U.N. agencies.

For a start, the incorporation of the word 'feminist' in our name claimed for Caribbean and other Third World women the right to focus on all the strategic issues facing women in our societies; issues which span the range of the social, economic, cultural, political and sexual. In addition, for Caribbean feminism as we sought to develop it, the emancipation of women and the transformation of exploitative social and environmental relations necessitated a clear challenge to the dominant world economic system and the development policies which emanated from it.

The period since our founding, 1985 to the present, has been one of great political and economic significance regionally and internationally. In many Caribbean countries, centre-right governments have pushed through economic reforms à la I.M.F. and the World Bank in a process now commonly known as 'structural adjustment'. These reforms, it is now agreed, have occasioned one of the largest transfers of wealth from the poor to the rich and from the South to the North in this century. The increased exploitation of women is central to these policies whether as the cheap 'unorganised' labour of Free Trade Zones, export processing zones, or as low cost service workers in an expanded tourism sector, or as the parents of last resort when rationalised or privatised health, education and other social services move beyond their reach.

Not surprisingly, therefore, it is the women of this region who have put up some of the fiercest battles against these policies (see CAFRA NEWS, Vol. 2, No. 2 and Vol. 3, No. 3). Work within CAFRA over this period has thus tended to reflect both the actions and struggles against these policies and the strength and creative power of women in their day-to-day survival. This creative power is shown in their cultural and artistic expression as well as in the fashioning, albeit on a small scale, of viable economic alternatives.

For example, an important area of CAFRA's work has been a programme of research and action on 'Women in Caribbean Agriculture' (WICA), a programme developed with the assistance of the Centro de Investigatión para la Acción Feminina (CIPAF) of the Dominican Republic and carried out initially in the Commonwealth of Dominica and St. Vincent and the

Grenadines. The programme is currently being extended to Belize and Trinidad and Tobago. This WICA experience presents one example of the methodology which has been developed over these years. The actual research challenges accepted definitions of women's work and attempts to develop new indicators for its measurement. At the same time, the collection of in-depth oral history interviews and their eventual publication will provide literary testimony of the relationship between the women agriculturalists' work and other aspects of their lives. Further, action programmes are being collectively forged out of the analysis by the researchers, the network of organizations involved and the communities in which the research was conducted.

Interestingly, researcher/activists of the WICA project, along with women, identified by CAFRA's Women's History and Creative Expression' project, joined a number of contributors to Creation Fire in our first Creative Writing Seminar in Trinidad and Tobago in May 1989. The rich outpourings of poetry, prose and oral history were grounded in the reality of Caribbean women's experiences and encapsulated a vision of change.

As our organization grows and our networks expand, we move into new but equally challenging areas. One such is 'Women and the Law', which will explore the issues related to women's rights and legal services. In this, as in all our activities, the development of popular forms of communication theatre, audio-visuals, cartoons, exhibitions and popular publications will be an integral part.

This publication and the other literary anthologies which we hope will follow in its wake (short stories, oral testimonies) is an example of our efforts to share and communicate, rising above geopolitical, historical, cultural, ethnic, linguistic, economic geographic and other barriers. But it is more than this. This anthology is a tribute to the vision of CAFRA members that:

> *poems are eternal rebels against all social relations since these must be contractual arrangements of power which are always to the advantage of some elite and therefore causing misery in the hearts of the people (the home of poems)*
>
> *They are considered inconsequential, but they have brought down governments (starting with the ones in our heads)...*

Nan Peacocke, *"About Poems"*
Creation Fire

It is also a tribute to all the struggling women poets of the region whose need for poetic expression transcends all the forces which would negate it.

Rawwida Baksh-Soodeen
Rhoda Reddock
CAFRA
Secretariat Members
September 1989.

Contents

The Mother   59

The Lover   85

The Exile   125

INTRODUCTION

Somewhere in Suriname, late at night or very early in the morning, a woman is sitting in a room alone, writing. Somewhere in Guyana another woman sits, doing exactly the same thing. The woman writes fiercely, compulsively, for many hours even though she is exhausted and sleepy and even though she has no immediate plan for her writing. She writes because she must. She is writing for her life. And in other parts of the Caribbean too — Trinidad, Curacao, St. Lucia, Jamaica, Barbados — throughout the archipelago all the way to Belize, and further down into South America, women are writing themselves into being. They write because the time has come when they must invent their new world.

This anthology, *Creation Fire*, is a collection of the work of such writers. It focuses upon their poetry. It has brought their voices together so that they can articulate a shared history which is Caribbean in nature. The majority of poets collected in this anthology do not yet have enough poetry for individual collections. Their poetry might easily have ended up in shoeboxes or among recipe collections, while they continued to attend, out of necessity, love or habit, to women's work in the Region. Bringing them together in published form provides a context for their work and valorizes it so that it attains a reality, separate from themselves, in print.

The Background

The idea of such an anthology was born at the launching of CAFRA as an association in 1985. The formation of an association dedicated to feminist research and action was an exciting and thrilling one. The event took place in April 1985 immediately following a regional meeting celebrating the end of the U.N. Decade for Women at WAND (Women and Development Unit of the Extra-Mural Department of the University of the West Indies) in Barbados. This meeting had been hosted jointly by WAND, the Women and Development Office of UN/ECLAC (United Nations/ Economic Commission for Latin America and the Caribbean) and CARIWA and brought together women from all over the Caribbean in a wide variety of women's organizations. To mark the birth of CAFRA many women spontaneously wrote poetry. It was there that the idea of an anthology of poetry as one of CAFRA's first projects was born. The realization of the project, however, has taken a long time. Part of the reason was that we attempted to do this with only a minimal budget, relying mainly upon the goodwill of our sisters in the Region and beyond. And the goodwill was there, in full measure, attesting to the strengths and the shared goals in the women's movement throughout the diverse countries of the Caribbean.

The Collection Process

But it was not easy to persuade the women of the Region to submit poetry. The number of recognized women poets of the Caribbean can be counted on one's fingers. Who then were these new writers whom CAFRA was seeking? It was difficult to find them, to convince them that the anthology was a serious and legitimate product, and to surmount the obstacle of their shyness. Our first call for submissions in July 1986 brought only a trickle of poems — about fifty altogether. But we knew that many more women were writing — I, for one, had been travelling throughout the Caribbean doing literary research and had met many, many would-be women writers. And at the WAND celebration at which CAFRA was launched, the Women's Cultural Workshop was very large and yielded a great deal of information about women's writing. It was clear that we were not yet reaching the majority of would-be contributors.

The problem seemed to be one of context. Women writers everywhere have the common problem of not taking themselves or their task so seriously that they give it pre-eminence over all other activities. And in the Caribbean the habit of publishing is absent because there is little access. It seemed that there was a necessity to bridge the gap between the writers' perceptions of themselves as dabblers in "a little poetry" and the labelling of themselves as poets and writers. I wrote an essay on context which was published in *CAFRA NEWS* and which is partly reproduced here.

> *Recent research throughout the Caribbean region reveals that there are many more struggling literary females than the printed output would lead us to believe. And, invariably, the product is poetry. It is not difficult to understand why. It is easier, after all, to write a poem if one has a few minutes between cooking, looking after children and coping with housework than a novel or a play. But much of this poetry is "silent" in that it remains private, unobtrusive, closeted. The practitioners of this art are not led to take themselves or their poems seriously and as a result the writing is sporadic, lacking in development, and eventually goes nowhere.*
>
> *It is important to note, though, that if women do not articulate and explore their own experience, their development cannot help but be stultified. Allowing one's insights to pass into the common pool of literary endeavour is part of the process of exchange in which human beings are engaged. It is in the interest of redressing this perceived deficiency in the publication of women's poetry in the Caribbean that CAFRA has initiated the task of compiling an anthology of contemporary poetry. The problem of writing and publishing is compounded by our history of slavery and indentureship, colonialism and its attendant disabling mechanisms. This applies of course to all writers, but more so to the women among them and especially to those women who have neither the means nor the circumstances to engage in creative activity for prolonged periods of time.*
>
> *(CAFRA NEWS, Vol I, #1, Mar.1987)*

This essay, together with other information about CAFRA and about the purpose of such an anthology, formed the basis of a kit which we distributed throughout the Region. Because of CAFRA's wide and diverse base, word about the anthology spread in a manner which transcended the barriers of race and class.

But I believe that the most significant transition was made in the minds of women who were writing in that they were able to place themselves in the context of something which was whole and integral to the Region, and to feel that their words would resonate together as a Caribbean voice rather than as an inconspicuous murmur in a large sea of writing by more important people. And this to me is the major achievement of the anthology. Unlike conventional works of this nature, it does not focus upon the individual. It speaks as a voice of the Region — giving expression to the major concerns, hopes and dreams of the women who inhabit this archipelago. The organizing principle of the work reflects this focus since the concerns and not the individuals form the basis for categorization. When the contributions started to roll in, we were amazed. For all of the efforts made, no one expected such a torrential array of poetry. Over 500 poems were received and the editorial committee was hard put to make the final selection. All of the poetry received was important, valid and creative. They all made statements about the sisters of the Caribbean and about the song and grief in their hearts. They were rich in that Caribbean music which has been forged out of the suffering and the jealously-hoarded joys of a people of great spirit. The poetry hummed with a blend of different voices, different races, different experiences. They came from within the Region and beyond, from North America and Europe from sisters who were now resident there but who had not cut the umbilical cord.

An important consideration is that this anthology does not, in any way, set out to be a comprehensive survey of Caribbean women poets or even a selected collection. Such poems as are included here were direct responses to our calls for submissions. Later, invitations were sent out to published poets of Caribbean origin who were known to us. The anthology makes a political and unambiguously feminist statement about its purpose and it would have been naive of us to expect all the invitees to respond. That the majority of them saw fit to do so makes its own statement about political commitment and feminism in the Region.

The Selection

As the editorial committee began the selection process, two things became apparent very quickly. One was that none of us wanted to lose any of this poetry although it was clear that it could not all be published. It was an important historical record. The other thing was that although the call for submissions never mentioned subject areas, similar themes were emerging over and over. We solved these problems in the following ways:

(i)   We decided to select for publication the poetry which would go into this volume, *CREATION FIRE*. Then, as an invaluable historical record, we would produce a limited edition publication of all of the poems which had been submitted.

(ii) We grouped the poetry into categories and out of this process was born the idea of arranging the poetry into themes. No effort was made to conceptualize the themes beforehand. They arose organically out of the mass of poetry lying in front of us and provided a forum for the articulation of these various Caribbean voices.

The editorial committee spent many months making the selection. At its largest it comprised eight people, half of whom were practising poets, some who were critics and others who simply read for pleasure. There were individual selections, group discussions, readings, and exclamations of astonishment, pain or "yes man!", as we participated in the collective selection process. In the final stages, the editorial eye was called upon to make harsh or difficult decisions and I take full responsibility for any untoward inclusions or omissions which might appear to readers.

The Themes

The theme which emerged most clearly as the overall preoccupation of the poets was that of resistance. Whether they were talking about love, sexuality, childbirth or their relationship to land and country, their overriding concern was the sense of being resistant to adversity from all quarters and, beyond that, to the act of translating this recognition of adversity into active combat with the forces which they perceived as threatening. These forces took on a multi-hued dimension. They included the forces of imperialism and American domination of the Region in cultural and other ways, sexism and the dominance of the patriarchal culture, the onslaught of the multinationals and so on... Not surprisingly, the largest sections were those entitled *The Region* and *The Guerrilla*. There were not as many poems about motherhood as we might have expected, especially since so many Caribbean women are single heads of households. Is it that motherhood is too difficult a subject to write about? Is it too mundane? Or somehow too close to home? The poetry provides a variety of questions without answers. Political issues seemed to be more important to these writers and there emerged strongly that embattled sense of surviving in the face of great and monumental odds, and being at war with forces larger than the individual and larger by far than the family unit.

The Seer is the voice of the seer-woman in our midst. It is both prophetic and historical as it ranges through the wealth of experience amassed in this archipelago and reminisces, restructures or chastises. It is foreseeing and warning - the reflective voice of our earliest mothers and our youngest daughters joined together.

The Artist searches for the sources of her being as she struggles to understand and control the creativity which she has no power to abandon in spite of its great cost. How to write, what is writing, where is the "home of poems" and how does the poet find her voice are some of the questions raised. The artist as a subversive societal figure is a very strong motif here, evoking images of the diablesse and other folk figures and the woman with special powers.

The Lover writes love poetry, some of which is not like love at all. Some of it is indeed tender, passionate, committed and erotic. But some of it is poetic verse of the sheerest rage, seething with that unbound anger that women often feel during a relationship with a lover. It protests against "licks" (battering) and rails against infidelity. For all of that, it remains poetry which is deeply engaged in the complex act of loving.

The Mother reflects upon mothering and being mothered. It encompasses the act of giving birth, raw nerves, economic hardship and delight. It is a fact of life for most Caribbean women, a lonely fact for many.

The Exile underlines the sense of an archipelago which has transcended national boundaries and which relates more deeply to a common history and geography of the spirit. It speaks movingly of the sensibility of Caribbean women in the metropoles, of their need for community, of their nostalgia for their permanent landscapes of the heart, of their undirected fears and their loneliness.

The Mourner is a relatively small section. It is reflective and religious, for the most part, and is concerned with reconciliation to an inevitable loss rather than with grief or rage at the inevitable force of death.

The Land shows the poets' concern with the geopolitics of their own countries. The voices are localized and passionate about issues in their own backyards. They show the deep attachment these poets have to the portion of the earth which they claim as their own. They state that while we claim the entire globe, as we have every right to do, we also claim our own yards. And in your own yard you must have sovereignty. Everyone needs that.

The Region is passionate about issues of regional freedom and independence. It is a voice that instinctively coalesces into a spirit of togetherness without the necessity for regulation and politically-worked solutions to the problems of unity. It divests itself of national boundaries as it estimates the costs, and quantifies the new bargains to be struck with those who still wield the power. It "cuts through fine white foam" like a "nib" of the greatest sensitivity as it makes us aware of our need to assert our common heritage and to plan our common destiny.

The Guerrilla is the largest section of this anthology. It is indeed a marvel that these diverse poets, working in individual cells, as it were, have arrived at a common point of utmost resistance to all the forces which have oppressed them for centuries. A strong cry of protest rises from these pages, but it is protest merged with action. The fighting spirit of the Caribbean woman proclaims itself as it celebrates the self and the Region worth fighting for.

The Worker is the smallest section. It is an ironical and very revealing comment on the attitudes of the poets to work. There are few women anywhere who work as hard as Caribbean women, whether in the home or out of it or, as is more often the case, in both. This is probably taken for granted as one of the mundane factors of existence. It is not a major source of poetic thought in this anthology.

The Survivor follows naturally from the mightily expressed struggles of the last few sections. It is the voice of endurance against a multitude of evils ranging from estate rape to colonization to domination by husbands and other males. But there is no resignation here, only courage, resilience and a boundless will to survive.

The Praise-Singer celebrates the beauty and the ferocity of the women of the Caribbean. It is sometimes abstract, sometimes purely ideological, running almost to cant, at other times it is simply reverential. It explores the important dimension of women talking to themselves and singing praise-songs in sisterhood and solidarity about each other and the place that they inhabit together.

The Contributors

The diverse mixture of race, class, language and culture existent in the Caribbean is reflected in this work. However, no attempt was made either in soliciting contributions or in the selection process, to represent the varied populations of the Region in proportion to their percentages in the different territories. This is, in the first place, an exceedingly contrived and difficult task for an editor, since different historical, sociological and cultural circumstances relative to producing poetry vary within the different ethnic groups. I can arrive at no generalities to describe these conditions as they impacted upon the anthology because each country has its own peculiarities and the emergence of a person engaged in the lonely act of writing poetry is unpredictable, at best. Yet there is no doubt that, throughout the Caribbean Region, the correlation of privilege (time, money, education, social status and political power) with race and class exists in full measure. Because of the unique search for poets undertaken in the collection of poetry published here, however, I believe that the voices of a number of groups previously unrepresented in Caribbean collections have emerged. One example of this is the voice of the Indian woman poet in Suriname, Guyana, and Trinidad and Tobago. CAFRA's present strength in membership lies in the English-speaking Caribbean. But there are also members in the French, Spanish and Dutch territories. The contributions reflect this because the overwhelming quantity of the poetry is written in English. But the contributions in languages other than English, although small, are signals of the feeling of commonality experienced by the women of the Region. We can see here the beginnings of a female crossing of the barriers of race, class, language and history, which have existed among us for the chief benefit of the colonizer. Glosses have been provided as adequately as was possible. It would have been ideal for each poet to supply a translation which was satisfactory to her, and this was the first method tried, but, on the whole, this was not the case. The glosses have concentrated upon providing meaning and not upon an attempt to render the work into a facsimile of English poetry.

The Poetic

For me, one of the literary rewards of editing this anthology was the sense of discovering the voice of the Caribbean woman: that voice unselfconsciousness and not engaged in any performance except that of personal introspection. The majority of these writers wrote for self, not expecting to be published, many, many of them stymied by the problem of *how* to become a poet. And in some indefinable way, because their acts of writing were so private and self-contained, they were speaking an important poetic truth about their experience. And so the anthology breaks through an almost impenetrable wall of silence lying between those few who speak and the mass of women whose lives consist simply of doing. It also speaks of a new vision of sisterhood which is becoming felt throughout the Caribbean, and which has great potential for resisting domination and division. This kind of sisterhood concentrates upon *commonweal*. It concerns itself with things, that are perhaps too important to that intimate sense of self which is our motivating force, for our politicians and persons of affairs to begin to address — the inner being, the future of humanity and the texture of our daily lives. It speaks not to issues of conquest nor to armies clashing in the night. It fastens itself on to ideas of harmony, life-enhancement and to the future of life itself.

An important consideration in beginning the discussion about Caribbean feminist poetics is the fact that our literary canon, such as it is, consists overwhelmingly of male writers. For emerging Caribbean women writers there are few theoretical models. The writers may be divided into major writers — Naipaul, Lamming, Harris (Wilson), Walcott and Braithwaite; and new writers — from new wave writing in the 1980s out of which voices like Kincaid, Cliff, Goodison, Senior and Harris (Claire) have emerged. Jean Rhys is an obvious exception to this although up to the mid-1970s she was not considered a West Indian writer by the majority of critics. It was apparent that the new women writers lived outside of the Caribbean, for the most part, or had lived abroad for many years, or were able to travel regularly. Our concern in CAFRA was for the voices which lay dormant in the region — struggling to find utterance, producing hidden writing or composing in their heads songs, poems and stories which were still unwritten. We sought originally to reach the so-called "grassroots-constituency", but soon discovered that the "unrepresented voice" transcended the barriers of race, class and language.

The collective voice in *Creation Fire* is strong and resonant — Audre Lorde speaks from her home in the U.S. Virgin Islands and a peasant woman on a farm in Suriname answers; Lorna Goodison speaks from Jamaica of the experience of *The Survivor* and an echo emerges from the cane-fields of Guyana or Trinidad or from the urban ghettoes of Brixton or L.A. There are poems begun in the minor key, like calypso's first tentative beginnings, but developing into full orchestral resonance in some cases and, in others, keeping the minor key intact. The poems in the anthology contain all the stages of the poetic process: from simile to full-bodied metaphor, replicating women's lives in transition.

In terms of the literary canon, this anthology contributes to an emerging feminist poetic which is peculiarly Caribbean. If the literature of the Caribbean is a strong but minor voice in that present body of world literature written in English, within that context the female writer's voice is still heard in the minor key. It seems clear though, that the Caribbean feminist poetic (feminist used in the absolute sense of empowering women) contributes something distinctively woman-centred to the Caribbean literary canon, and something distinctively Caribbean-centred to the global feminist poetic and to global feminism as a whole. A different ethos governs this nascent Caribbean feminist poetic and it concerns women's relations with men. Gender separateness is perceived differently from that of women in countries such as North America and Europe because while their men (fathers, brothers, sons, lovers) are safe, no such assurances are available for Caribbean and other Third World women, and most particularly, for such women living in the region now known as the Fourth World. Perhaps for these very reasons, we find subsumed in our literary texts, a unique feminist political agenda. To some extent this might explain the rootedness of the warrior theme in an anthology such as this one.

The overflow of women's writing in this decade parallels the intensive development of the women's movement in the Caribbean. This is not to say that the writing can be attributed to the growth of the women's movement in a direct way, but some correlation can be made, I believe, between the restructuring of the level of dialogue in the public sphere to include women's issues on a wide scale, and the new creative output of women writers. For example, the treatment of women in the calypso of the latter part of the 1980s in Trinidad and Tobago is markedly different from that of earlier periods in terms of the respect, dignity and personhood accorded to women. It is prudent, though, to view development and creative leaps as occurring in sets of parallel sequences instead of relating them to causal factors in a linear way. This would seem to be the case in the Caribbean where a general conscientization of women seems to have taken place on many fronts at once.

The "Tree of Life", a batik painting by Sharon Chacko, answered the book's title so well that their coming together seemed much more than coincidental. It was coincidental in that it was not commissioned as a cover, but its essential artistic statement is very much at the core of what this anthology sets out to do in its intention to see the processes of living in a holistic manner with no artificially-imposed divisions upon mind, body and spirit. The woman's healing and procreative power is physical and primal on one level, and equally vast and creative upon every other level. And so that fire of creation extends, as in the anthology, to the power of protest and action and the varied strategies of resistance to all of the forces of domination.

How far, asked one of the contributors, does this anthology challenge the traditional notion of what is poetry? The reader must judge that because I can find no ready means of estimating such a departure. Poetry is, in fact, the most rebellious and unconventional of forms, constantly seeking new breakwaters and unearthing strange harmonies. Some of the contributors work in the dub medium, for example, Jean Binta Breeze and Ahdri Zhina Mandiela. And each country produces its own special idiom and its unending varieties of that same idiom. So the anthology reflects the poetic sensibility of the contemporary twentieth century world, approaching the agonies of our own fin-de-siècle, with a Caribbean centre. Some of the voices are tentative, some strident, some assured. Some are the voices of schoolgirls who show as yet undeveloped potential, and some are older women with dreams of writing channelled, out of necessity, into other familial enterprises, but resurrected for this anthology.

For me, as editor of the work, by far the most moving experience has been the direct interaction with the poets after reading their poetry. This has occurred in a variety of ways — through correspondence, telephone calls, personal notes appended to biographical data forms, and personal contacts. It is exciting and gratifying to be part of a nascent movement towards a Caribbean feminist poetic. In spite of our many differences, we share each other's common "lash" in this great archipelago of the spirit.

Recently, I listened to Derek Walcott talking about the process involved in his poetic development. Finding his own voice was, of course, the most important part of the search. And in attempting to explain how his hybrid voice became stronger and stronger as he learnt to integrate the rhythms and realities of his earliest self into what was becoming an increasingly complex and highly refractive verse form, he sums up: "I have always written to the melody of my own voice."

Defining a poetic sensibility which is specifically Caribbean as distinct from a North American, European, Commonwealth, African or Indian poetic is a very hazardous and difficult thing to attempt to do. Yet it is necessary to attempt to do things like these because such a quotient exists and if we understand it well, it can serve as a jumping-off point for issues far more earth-shattering than poetry. For a Caribbean reality exists and because we have been nurtured within its fold, we know its depths as naturally and intimately as we know the sound of our mother's voice. It is my belief that such a fertile accumulation of poetic experience cannot but reproduce itself. The emergence of *new women poets*, engaged in sustained acts of writing, is one of the positive future projections of this anthology.

RAMABAI ESPINET
Toronto, 1989.

CREATION
FIRE

The Seer

Jean Binta Breeze

DREAMER

roun a rock corner
by de sea
seat up
pon a drif wood
yuh can fine she
gazin cross de water
a stick
eena her han
trying to trace
a future
in de san

Audre Lorde

NEVER TO DREAM OF SPIDERS

Time evaporates
between the lips of strangers
days collapse into a hollow tube
and soon implodes against now
like an iron wall
my eyes are blocked with rubble
smears of perspective
blurring each horizon
In the breathless precision of silence
a malignant word is made.

Once the renegade flesh was gone
fall air lay against my face
sharp and blue as a needle
but rain fell through October
and death lay   a condemnation
within my blood.

The smell of your neck in August
a fine gold wire bejewelling war
all the rest lies
illusive as a farmhouse
on the other side of the valley
vanishing in a humid afternoon.

Day three   day four   day ten
the seventh step   a veiled door
leading to my golden anniversary
flame-proof free-paper shredded
in the teeth of a pillaging dog

Never to dream of spiders

And when they turned the hoses upon me
a burst of light.

JUDITHS FANCY

Half-built
your great-house looms
between me and the sun
shell-smells on the morning wind
you are younger than my daughter
your little boy is blonde
the moon is new
my sloping land brings our eyes level
"Welcome, neighbor" I begin.

Did I oppress you in another life
or do your eyes always turn to flint
on meeting a Black woman
face to face?

Your child speaks first
"I don't like you" he cries
"Are you coming to babysit me?"

Kamla Best

L'ETRE

I have cracked my
last skin;
this is my ninth life,
my final season,
fall.
I will never forgive
your greatness,
your infinite explosions,
for now there is no
room left
in my silent vessel
where I find peace

CE MAL

this is the book
of silences,
of people dressed
in soft, edged voices;
of eyes that never look
up. These are
the same ringed
eyes that watched
me grow old.
This is the same
voice,
the voice that
now rises on a
fall.

Aimée Eloidin

TEL EST NOTRE VIEUX MONDE!

Un jour vient de mourir.
Un autre naît déjà!
Tel est notre univers
Vieux d'années et de siècles.
Fatigué et usé par cette vie passée
Déchiré, déchiqueté par cette vie agitée.
Tel est notre vieux monde!
Usé et lessivé par ces heures immondes
Agonisant lentement, criant grâce ou pitié!
Tel un vieil homme usé qu'un mal secret ronge
Qui s'accoche à la vie et pense toujours au songe
Se traîne sans dignité pour implorer sa grâce
Se traîne dans la boue et tache de crasse.
Des pustules dégoutants couvrent son épiderme
Tandis que de sa bouche sort un flot de blasphèmes!
Ses membres squelettiques refusent obéissance
À cet être qui n'a plus ni sens, ni décence.
Tel est notre vieux monde!
Un vieil homme dégoutant qui s'en va vers la tombe.

SUCH IS THIS OLD WORLD OF OURS

A day has just died
Already another is born
Such is our universe
Years, centuries old,
Fatigued, worn out by this life it has led
Torn, ripped apart by this busy life,
Such is this old world of ours!
Worn out, washed out by these squalid hours
A slow misery, crying out for mercy or pity!
Like a worn-out old man whom a secret sickness devours
Who hangs onto life and still dreams his dream
Crawls about without dignity to beg for mercy
Crawls about in the mud and filth
Disgusting sores cover his skin
And out of his mouth comes a steady stream of curses
His skeleton limbs refuse to obey
Such is this old world of ours,
A disgusting old man en route to his grave.

Afua Cooper

TO KHETIWE

So sista
you ask me
what can a woman who likes being big
a woman who enjoys her size
do when other sistas make unfavourable comments about
it and coyly suggest weight-loss clinic
"it's not easy being a fat Black woman," you say

I can make a few suggestions
potential replies to throw back at these mahgah women
first tell them that you are into yourself
and because you are into yourself
you're not a slave to fashion
not a slave of babylon
then tell them that thin
might be in
but fat is no sin
next, ask if they know of their ancient traditions
that in southeastern Nigeria
the rich and not so rich used to send their daughters
to Old Calabar to make them beautiful
beautiful in this case meant
fat
        plump
above size 12

Lima Fabien

INTROSPECTION

Je cherche enfin la nuit
Cent fois décrite en thême
Je cherche mon oubli
En moi s'est assoupi
Je cherche sans connaitre
Par mon intuition sans doûte
Dessus leur instruction
Incarnée par mon maître
Insatiable sans fin
En bas c'est la défaite
C'est ici mon destin
Je cherche la raison
Ternie et sans égale
Fugitive à chaque mot
Et qui connait mon mal
Je cherche tout en parole
La rage d'une douleur
Quand dans la marge enfin
Quand sur la page pleine
S'inscrivent des messages d'amour
Que je souffre encore d'un karma, d'une bataille
Sur mon chemin soudain s'effacent les détails
C'est ici mon chemin soudain s'effacent les details
C'est ici mon destin
C'est ici qu'au matin
C'est ici que demain...
Je frappe à chaque porte
Personne, les voix se meurent
Je frappe et je colporte
Aux regards clos des deumeures
Je cherche ainsi la vie que j'avais oublié
Je cherche ainsi l'envie de cesser de pleurer
Je frappe quand j'ai mal et que je dois m'enfuir
Le doigt sur la conscience enracinée dans la terre foulée de mon empire
Je frappe comme je dois
Devant l'ame indiscrête
Je frappe dans mon émoi

Aujourd'hui je suis prête
Je m'etais impréniée de la porte interdite...
Où tout s'est emmélé
J'ai souri à l'enfant
En plein sur la montagne
Me suis enfuie du bagne
De mon foetus naissant
Je vous ai vu prier.

INTROSPECTION

Finally I seek the night
Focus of too many descriptions
I seek my forgetting
so long sleeping within
I search without knowing
by intuition no doubt
Above their teachings
Embodied by my master
insatiable without end
I seek reason
Tarnished and without equal
Eluding every word
and which knows my pain
I seek everything through words
The rage of a pain
When finally
    in the margin
    on the filled page
messages of love are written:
That I still suffer from a karma, from a battle
Suddenly the details of my passage disappear
Here is my passage
Here is my destiny
And here, in the morning
And here, tomorrow...
I knock on each door
No one there, voices die away
I knock and I peddle my wares
beneath the closed gaze of the houses
See how I seek the life I'd forgotten
See how I seek the desire to stop weeping
I knock when I suffer and I must flee myself
My finger on a conscience rooted in the trampled earth of my
empire
I knock as I must

Before the indiscrete soul
I knock in my upheaval
Today I am ready
I impregnated   the forbidden door
Where everything was tangled up
I smiled right at the child
on the mountain
I fled the hard labour
of my burgeoning foetus
I saw you pray.

C. Carrilho-Fazal Ali-Khan

POEM

Ben ik op zoek
naar iets
waarvan ik de naam
niet weet

tederheid
beheerst mijn dromen
een blik, een gebaar
meer een voelen
en weten
we kennen elkaar

POEM

In search am I
of something
I do not know
the name of

tenderness
sways my dreams
a look, a gesture
rather a feeling
and knowing
we know each other

Lima Fabien

RENCONTRE DANS LA NUIT

Un soir, une onde enfouie dans les néons de mon esprit
Sortant de ma torpeur que j'avais pourchassé
Hantant ma vie je pense le flambeau à la main
Privée de désarroi comme un parfum léger d'une onde
ensorcelée
Privée des mots si simples par sa bouche confies
L'étau dans une enceinte son coeur m'avait serré

Un soir, une onde mélange syllabique du jardin fatidique
M'empêchant de dormir juste en face de mes yeux murés et
éblouie
Où naquit Dieu un jour, vibration de l'amour, baignée dans la
lumière
Coiffée de la conscience qu'elle m'avait emprunté innocente,
naïve
De son corps dépouillé elle s'est déshabillée
Un soir, une onde clamant sa délivrance vint briser tout le
charme
Chimérique destin, je flottais sur les eaux
Onirique tremplin, du sein de mon enfance caressé de sa main
N'ayant plus peur de rien, n'ayant plus peur du temps
Silhouette maternelle à la vie s'étant plainte
Tranchée par la rosée jamais ne m'a revu quand j'avais les
mains jointes

Un soir, une onde toute la vie sans doûte, toute la nuit durant
Elle m'a montré la route a parlé des enfants
Fondant ses étamines sépales et auréoles
Enivrant le pistil émanant de ma vie
Chatouillant mon esprit qui s'attriste soudain

Une onde m'est venue caressant mes tympans
Dans une ronde farfelues, c'était le temps sans temps.

NIGHT ENCOUNTER

One evening, a wave buried in the neons of my spirit
Out of the torpor that I'd chased away
Haunting my life I think a torch in my hand
Deprived of disorder like the wafting perfume of a bewitched
wave
Deprived of those words so simple confided by her mouth
Vicegrip her heart surrounded me on all sides

One evening, a wave syllabic assortment of the fateful garden
Keeping me from sleeping before my walled and dazzled eyes
Where God one day was born, vibration of love, bathed in light
Coiffed in the consciousness that she loaned to me innocent,
naive
She shed the garment of her naked body
One evening, a wave demanding deliverance came and broke
the spell
A chimera of destiny, I floated on the waters
Springboard for dreams, of my childhood breast caressed by
her hand
No longer fearing anything, no longer fearing time
The maternal silhouette having complained to life
Cut short by the dew never saw me again when I had clasped
hands

One evening, a wave my whole life no doubt, the entire night
She showed me the road, spoke of children
Melting her stamens, sepals and halos
Intoxicating the pistil emanating from my life
Tickling my soul which suddenly is saddened

A wave came to me caressing my eardrums
In a farfetched dance, it was time without time.

Sharon Lee Wah

EXPERIENCES

I have not had much experience
    Of falling in love, of getting drunk
I have had a few experiences
    But they don't add up to much... experience.

Yet this have I had, I've smelt, I've touched,
    I've seen the brilliance of a colour-streaked sky
    at sunset
    I've felt the shock, the thrill, that unsettling,
    itching feeling
    that disturbed the surface of my being, my
    equilibrium,
    almost like swallowing sea-water
    and getting your ears suddenly deafened

This have I had
the silver stars at sunset
the coolness of the afternoon
the sweetness of the rain on my hands

This have I had
a poem of life and remembrance
of a presence long gone
a silent evening of fellowship
when young hearts beat as one

No, I have not had much experience
Yet I have had these experiences
And though there are wasted moments
The empty hours of loneliness
the sensation of young life going by
unused, unlived, untried
Although it's this kind of experience
as well as the other
That make up my stock of moments of feeling,
I will cherish all my experiences
Such experiences as I have had.

Nneka

REFLECTIONS

(for Fleckin' & Rodney)

Remember may june '76 when the cracklin
brown leaves were there on the ground
the poui bloomed yellow flame
and we were all happy together
studying, lovin' and feeling' mellow
although exams were on their way
and although I was convinced I'd fail
still overslept, did political work
argued politics instead of beat, beat, beat
in the enclave among those trees
raised in prayer to the moon.

There were walks to Papine in the night
for endless cornbread and cheese
washed down with orange drink
coffee stops at Seacole or Taylor
you writing a bloody great thesis
Rodney smoking half & half
underlining precedents in his note books
while I slept on the desk over
'Socialism and The Newly Independent States!'

And life was sweet
Although there was curfew in the city
and man and man, was a dead.

We were too happy.

Yvone Mechtelli Tjin-a-Sie

POEM

I.

Een neger ben ik
tot in mijn ziel draag ik
de kleur van mijn voorvaderen
de winti's, de Gadoe's ben ik
Ik ben de kromanti, de apoekoe
de vodoe, de luangoe
de schepper van mijn voorvaderen
de schepper, mijn maker
heft de 'handen op
en zegent zijn creatie

II.

Vandaag
is eenzaamheid
de grootste vijand
waartegen ik vechten moet

of moet ik stilaan het beleven
berusten in mijn leven
dat elk mens niet heeft
hetzelfde lot
Vandaag
heb ik te gast
hij die niets zegt, niets vraagt
alleen maar duisternis en angst
achter de gesloten deuren laat

III.

Als een zon
in de duistere nacht
breek je na vreselijke weeen
de wereld binnen
spartelend groet je
en de wereld kijkt
kijkt naar je eerste stappen
voetje voor, voetje achter
kruip je steeds vooruit
lachend maar bijtend
op mijn vingers
zeg ik: "Je zult staan Revolutie
op beide benen
De wereld moet dat beleven".

POEM

I.
A black I am
even in my soul I bear
the colour of my forebears
the wintis, the Gaddoes I am
I am the cromanti, the apookoo
the voodoo, the luangoo
the creator of my forebears
the creator, my maker
raises his hands
and blesses his creation

II.

Today
loneliness is
the worst enemy
I have to fight

or am I to gradually live to see it
resigning to my life
that everyone does not have
the same fate

Today
my guest is
he who says nothing, asks nothing
leaving only darkness and fear
behind closed doors

III.

Like a sun
in the dark night
you break after dreadful throes
into the world
sprawling you greet
and the world looks
looks at your first steps
one foot forward, one foot after
you always crawl onward
laughing but biting
my fingers
I say: "You shall stand Revolution
on both feet
The world should live to see that".

Merle Collins

THE BUTTERFLY BORN

Something old
Something new
Something borrowed
Something blue

The caterpillar dead
The butterfly
born

Alé asiz anba tab-la!
Zòt fouten twop.[1]
Go an' siddown under de table!
You too fas'.
You tink it easy?
Even wid all o' dat

Wid de mudder shoutin'
In days long ago
Dat little girl
Used to walk two, three days a week
From St David's town
By the police station
Where she Mammie use to work
Right up to Sauteurs town
By de ball-pitch groun'
Afraid of she shadow
of de basket shadow
of she dress shadow
of de fig-leaf shadow
But walkin' alone
all kind o' hour
Hidin' an' cryin' an' hatin'
Becus she Mammie
couldn't afford it
An' to besides
Was really a waste
o' good money
To pay de bus a whole
eight pence ha'penny

De biggest girl of five
Walkin' to bring
de little piece o' bread
de two grain o' bluggoe
for Iona an' Joycelyn an' Jude
an' Stephen
To keep body an' soul togedder
Woman-chile
A giant of nine
Strong since den
Strong even when bathed
in tears
Strong when blisters formed
from walking
A strong
premature
nine-year-old mother

Part of the history
Part of de life
De strength inherited
De weakness taught
Something old
Something true

I
must remember dat day
when Auntie Iona come from
England
I
Hold on to de blin'
An' watch Mammie
in de sittin' room
An Auntie Iona
nice nice nice
Wid earring
an' stocking
an' lipstick
an' ting

Auntie
Auntie
Iona
Oh hello!
Isn't that
Antoinette?

An' Mammie
So vex she could bus'
She face
tellin' de story
Of dogs among doctors
Of little girl who
don' know dey place
An' I
squeezin back
behin'
de blin'
Not darin' to answer
One Ionic question
Lookin' straight
At Mammie face
An' slinkin' back

Behin'
de blin'

Den come
de eruption
De whispered
benediction
Clear out
Kadammit fout[2]
Children
must know dey place

An' especially
little girl
Somebody
talkin' to you?
Outside!
All you always dey
To make people shame

Something borrowed
Something
blue
Mother
Teaching
As she was taught
Little girls
Must learn
To be seen not heard
Or is certain
destruction
Is pillar of saltness
Oh God!
Look how Lot
smart
An' he wife
so fas'
A pillar of salt!

De lesson
passed on
Alé asiz anba tab-la
Zòt fouten twop
Dammit fout
Chile
Nuttin' good
Could come o' you
Little girl like you
Only rompin' an' runnin'
An' climbin' tree
Like dose little boy
Oh Jesus
De Lord
Give me a trial
An' is me
people go blame
Yuh know

Woman-chile
Crying for the world
Crying for me
Crying because
I couldn't find their Eve
Who
In times past
Has shouted
When told to whisper
And lived
To expose
De deadly truth
Dat de wages of sin
Is life
before death

Sa Ki fè'w?
Sa ou ka pléwe pou?
What wrong wid you?
What you cryin' for?
Vini tifi³
vini
vini
mwen Kay héle ba'w
I go bawl for you

Something
blue

23

Wid a leson
like dat
1979[4]
not no easy ting
But de strength was dey
De weakness imposed
De adventure was dey
De spirit just hushed
Now
woman-chile
woman
All of a sudden
Not under no table
But out in de open

Demanding equal
recognition
For equal beauty given

Something new
Something true

From
Zòt fouten twòp
You too fas'
To Woman step forward
To Woman
Equal in Defense
Huh
You tink it easy?

Something new
Something true

What that mean?
You think is a puzzle?
Something dead
Something born

But
De caterpillar's death
De butterfly's birth
Is only a miracle
If you doh know
de story
Is only a mystery
if you doh know the history
Is only truly
a puzzle
If you can't find
the pieces
If you can't explain
de changes

Is de beauty of science
if you follow
the history
Is the poetry of science
If you watch
de movement
Famn
Alé douvan
Woman
Step forward
Something new
Something true

The caterpillar dead
The butterfly born!

[1] *Patwa. Transalated in the two lines immediately following.*
[2] *Possibly a mixture of progressive Patwa 'ka', English 'dammit' and Patwa 'fout' meaning 'damn'.*
[3] *Patwa : Come, little girl.*
[4] *The New Jewel Movement came to power in Grenada on March 13th 1979*

Rutheen Taylor

ELECTION

two answers to the question
"What is the difference
between a pessimist
and an optimist?"

The Priest's answer

One says,
"Good Lord, morning!"
The other says,
"Good morning, Lord!"

The Poet's answer

Gravely solemn or blithely blest,
in somber gray or rainbows dressed,
to moan and dirge and threnody
or jigs' and reels' bright melody
go trodding march or tripping sway;
declare your stand, then greet the day.

Gladys do Rego-Kuster

POEM

M'a buskabu
den memoria di mi pueblo
graba pa mannan blanka
Ku leter preta
riba papel

M'a buskabu
den kurasou di nos patria
riba borchi
riba estatua
bida eterua p'esuan
K'a sobresali

M'a buskabu
den memoria di nos mama
plama mane chemene
den tur nachi
den tur skina
te ora m'a bin komproude
muhe
muhe
UNDA b'a keda?!

POEM

I searched
my people's memory
black graphics engraved
by white hands
on sheets of paper

I searched
my nation's soul
the streetnames
the statues
eternal life for those who excelled

I searched
my mother's memories
dispersed like soot
In every nook
and cranny
until I understood

woman
woman
what has become of you!

Jennifer Rahim

BEGINNING

Exiled upon this ledge
  I stand
naked with unknowing,
facing winds that blow
hurricanes within me.

Standing as I was held
(their world beginning where
mine ended)
shrivelled, wet and crying —
Mama why did you expel me,
left me abandoned upon this
ledge of
beginnings?

You smiled,
exulting in my newness
as I fumbled to train
uncertain steps
to balance on edges.

You said that learning
begins with falling off
of this ledge.

Imelda Valerianus-Fermina

MUHE

Hari, muhé, hari tira gargant atras,
Estei pará den bo balkon,
Kaba hari, drenta bo kamber
tapa barika bou riba bo kama bo yora.

Kaba yora, dal e kara un labá
Pasa peña den e kabel...
I sali djingueli asina enfrentá mundu.

Tira ayera tras di lomba
No pensa riba ayera, ya ta tardi,
Mañan si Dios duna bo bida
Ora bo mira e aurora
Di un dia nobo na horizonte.

Habri brasa p'e dia nobo
Bo n'sa kiko e ta trese
Pero bo mester aseptá,
Di pursi ta e mes un wega
Ku mundu ta hunga ku nos,
Nos ta hunga ku mundu.

WOMAN

Laugh, woman, rock with laughter,
while standing on your balcony,
having laughed, enter your room
And fall flat on your bed to cry.

Having cried, wash your face,
Comb your hair...
And leave refreshed to face the world.

Throw all yesterdays behind you,
Don't think of yesterday,
it's late afternoon already,
Tomorrow, if God wills it
You see the dawn
Of a new day at the horizon.

29

Embrace that new day,
You don't know what it will bring,
Yet accept, you must,
Actually, it's the same game
The world plays with us,
That we play with the world.

Belen Kock-Marchena

POEM

Bo tei.....felicidat?
ma buska bo
den tur hoeki
na kada skiná.
Ma ta con
bo a laga mi
kansa mi kurpa
tanto asina.
Ta un wega
bo kyer
a hunga
ku mi,
pa despues
bo laga mi
descubri
ku ta mi mes
tin e jabi
pa habri
e porta
y jama bo
bon bini?

POEM

Are you there happiness?
I have looked for you
In every nook
at every corner.
Why did you
make me
tire myself
so much.
Is it a game
you wanted
to play
with me
To afterwards
let me
discover
that I myself
have the key
to open
the door
and welcome
you.

Ushanda io Elima

WITHOUT AND WITHIN

i a woman without country
    save this earth and beyond
I belong to no race
    but Life's myriad forms
no community's mine
    save all who love Life

i-self have no-thing
    and yet All is ours
no one fully knows i
    still wholly i'm known
as no one am i
    and i'm Everyone

31

Leleti Tamu

ON A GREY DAY

The sky looks grey as the smoke from the factory blends easily
with it.
I can't feel the sun on this grey day, when leaves are no longer
green but overnight became orange, yellow, red, and brown

They look so very tired rain fell on them last night
It fell slow and soft the way my tears sometimes do.
This lonesome wetness used to soothe me, but last night they
seem to be the tears I left inside.

On a clear day I do see forever
But on a grey day with the sun sleeping through most of it

And the trees dying again, I look/feel tired and old without a
choice of orange, yellow, red, or brown just cold shades of grey.

Asha Radjkoemar

POEM I

o bloed
waarom ijl je
door mijn a'dren

o adem
waarom blaas je
door mijn longen

o vlees
hoe vervorm je
mijn lichaam

o geest
hoe ben je
in mij

hoe zijn jullie
in mij

terwijl
ik
nog ver
buiten
mezelf
ben

POEM I

o blood
why do you rush
through my veins

o breath
why do you blow
through my lungs

o flesh
how you deform
my body

o mind
how you are
in me

how are you
in me

while
I
am
still far
without
myself

Toni Vuurboom

I AM THE DOOR

Somewhere around Matura,
Along the Toco Road,
Three words are painted on the door
Of a humble abode.

They reassure the visitors
Seeking beaches bright,
And light the dark for travellers
Who walk into the night.

This little door is clearly not
The entrance to a mansion;
It's hardly smaller than its hut
Of straw with mud foundation.

Yet it bears for the world to see
Good tidings, like the dove
The words are few. So few, just three.
They tell us, 'God is Love*'.

Deuteronomy 6:9

Kiren Shoman

THEY LIKED ME THEN

They told me long ago: They told me
long before I could grasp any sense
of it. They told me so I'd grow up
with these thoughts of glory in my
mind as I matured.

So they told me of this great
being who lived in the sky, in
the clouds, and made sure no one
did wrong. I was scared stiff when
I lied to them and told them I
understood. They liked me then.

The Artist

Grace Nichols

OMEN

I require an omen, a signal
I kyan not work this craft
on my own strength
on my own strength

alligator teeth
and feathers
old root and powder

I kyan not work this craft
this magic black
on my own strength

Dahomey lurking in my shadows
Yoruba lurking in my shadows
Ashanti lurking in my shadows

I am confused
I lust for guidance
a signal, a small omen
perhaps a bird picking
at my roof

All is silent now
silent the fields
silent the canes
silent the drum
silent the blades
silent the sea
turning back to silence
a fatalistic rising silence

What's that sound/What's that flame?

Niala Maharaj

YOU AND I

Picture the diablesse,
Her back against the green, green,
Black-green of the forest,
Lurking in wait for our men.
Her frilled skirt covers that deformity,
The mark of power and corruption,
While we, in our backyards,
White flourbag aprons covering our domestic bellies,
Put loaves, with long poles, into earthen ovens
And hear the sound of village churchbells
Travelling on the wind.
She ranges the highways on a white decorative horse,
Driven madly by that power and weakness
Hidden under the frilled skirt.

You and I know instinctively of the evil
That pricks her on,
As she waits impatiently with the sound of owls and the rustle
of mongooses
Stalking prey among the dry leaves that cover the forest floor.

Snakes surround her also,
Twined around tree trunks and beckoning with eyes
That twinkle with laughter and joy.

The twinkle reflects in the eyes of the prey,
My husband,
His smooth black skin flushed after a night's carousing,
His young-old manhood weighing heavy with him
As he dares the forest path at midnight.

When the straight-backed rector and all other men
Are home asleep with their wives.
He looks around him, smelling danger on the wind.
His heart beats faster, and he spurs his horse on,
But tries to cover his fear with a whistle.
(It will make a good story to tell the others safely at home)
He beholds her with a jolt.
Her white frilled dress in the moonlight against the black, black
forest,
Her smile gentle and wild.
He had been expecting her all along,
Has come on this path just for her,
And we know it, too, which is why
He has received so many warnings,
So much evil conjured up
By our straight, tough, leathery tongues
That tell of fear,
Our fear.

The story ends, as it always does,
With escape.
He disentangles himself from the embrace
Though it tears his being as the forest branches
Tear at her frilly dress
When she paces among the wild animals and threatening
shadows,
Feeling the loss that he experienced briefly
Before fear/triumph/danger-recollected-in-tranquility took
over.

And when he returns with his smooth black skin and
mischievous
twinkle to me,
Of the dark skirt and white apron and closed face
And obscene thoughts,
What then of the diablesse,
As she sadly closes the file on this victim
And starts preparing for the next prospect.
As she repairs her make-up and mends her skirt
In the dry daylight when the forest is no longer black
And she no longer a myth to be feared,
Does she then, maybe,
Sit down and write poetry?

Kamla Best

ON SEARCHING FOR A MUSE

I. On Searching for a Muse

Assuming visions of a
lost land
of an exile;
moved by images of old
faces
reflected in the street.
Wondering about the next
step your blackened
sneaker will take into
the early morning;
The dark people
of dark poems
we spent the year with
come back to you
bitter but not shaken
you turn the page

II. Amer

Later that evening you
turn,
watching the smoke curl into
the naked light;
You think of the eternal sea
spitting up tired skeletons.
You consider your past
as one about to die
or perhaps as one already
dead, stilled rather,
The absurdity strikes you
you smile, roll over
and sleep,
your light, and others'
against the smoggy
evening
like the white queens'
quarters.

III. Relapse

We were together that day
watching the waves
move us, watching us
as if apart, like pawns
play roles for the king
and queen;
Losing the thread
and searching
among smiles
and silent eyes
the echo of everything
made it all nothing;
we stood uttering words
neither of us understood
as we looked past
our eyes.

Opal Palmer Adisa

MY WORK SPEAKS OF THOSE OTHER WOMEN

I am
wo/man
I woo, I walk, I wail, I talk.

My poetry
are legs and breasts
thighs and swinging behinds;
the poems cry of neglect,
laugh with the sun
dance under the blazing flamboyant trees
raise dust with bare feet
and use the hem of dresses to wipe sweat,
wipe odor from brows and sweating underarms

These poems are women
reeking of the blood
that drips monthly
that some women put in their food
to keep what's theirs theirs
singing of troubles locked in the box
that females are always left to guard
these poems are about women
who have always worked
in soil, at river banks
in beds, in kitchens, on street corners
working without writing down their poems
working so that others can study and write about them
working because they must.

These poems are of the Shes.
She is there
for the supporting,
for the unplugged microphones,
to produce;
she is there
and gives birth to new poems
some stored in the after birth
some postponed/denied by the pill, the bush tea,
the condom, the withdrawal, the abortion;
these are Women's poems
defined by their roundness
their backs tall and hard;
their lips pulled tight
to quiet the scream.

These are female poems
wet with vaginal juice
and the loving eyes
that women keep for each other;
these poems are herstory.

Elaine Savory

PREMENSTRUAL

this poem is awkward
like this time of fullness
breasts most lovely
need to be lonely
am a pile of pins in chaos
dreams picture-book distracting
nothing connects

but the poems come easy
each their own character
& all full-term
& mysterious

temper all flares and differences
don't speak to me freely
hourly my mind has a new shape
& only in the far and quiet cave
of thinking
is there a chance for satisfactions

a week from now
the moon divines something other
i wake needing
to talk in kisses
mood level and willing

but it all comes to one
after a month of changes

i make
better
in this solitude from men
monthly seclusions
brought from the old proud time
pre-his
story

everything changes
except the adept machine
but since i am no made thing
of a man
never his object
slave for his inspiration
who says i can be one thing
and create?

Kiren Shoman

MY POEM

I sat down the other day
To write a poem,
And I was going
To write about love —
But it's too common.
So I tried to write about
God and Religion,
But that was quite boring.
I wrote a couple of verses on
Nature, but it was hard to
Decide what I really
Wanted to say,
WHAT I FELT.

I was confused.

So I started writing
about confusion. I wrote
about my being unsure
of myself.
But it was still an odd poem;
it was this.

Margaret Gill

CORRETJER[*]

(to Corretjer)

Who will speak the conscience
of your deepest island?
Who now to poet
the dreams for a freer people?
Corretjer, beyond visions,
beyond struggles,
May your deeper dreaming
be for agitation of new poets.

[*]*Corretjer: Puerto Rican nationalist poet and activist who died January 1985.*

Joy Mahabir

FIRE AND STEEL

I remember only
One night:
Nights of fever and beating
Brought us to this place.
Voices, stilled passion,
Movement in anticipation.
I remember only
One moment:
Steel bursting into sound
Sticks clenched in sweating hands
Now lacking, existing
In happenings I forget.
I remember only:
Intense union
Freeing, uplifting
Minutes of living
And after, I forgot.

Charmaine Gill

WHY

I write poetry
Because I'm black
And sometimes,
It's not enough
To swear,
Or throw my fist
Through a wall
When someone looks right
 Through me.

I write poetry
Because I'm in love
And sometimes
It's not enough
To paint a picture
Unless I use
A thousand words.

I write poetry
Because I'm afraid
To dive into the wreckage
And find that there's not enough
to say what I really mean.

DEAR JONES

The brave never write poetry,
They find strength in anonymity.
I read your book
The Brave Never Write Poetry
And fell in love
With your alcoholism,
Your bisexuality,
Your suicidal tendencies,
Your life.
You are my mirror image.
My being is reflected in your eyes.
We're not brave,
but
We are anonymous.

Ramabai Espinet

MAMA GLO

I am fertile now
Rivers of creative memory
Running
Through my veins
Finding
The streams of my own voice
Dread and wise
And unknown to me...

As if one morning
When there is
No hunger,
No sickness,
Only the fresh latch
Of dawn
Breaking open the nylon
Shutters of light,
Only the salt kiss
Of waves
White and green
On the almond sand,

And I bend
Backwards
To the source
Coming for shelter
Coming for knowing
Coming to find

There is a roaring
In my head
Rivers of words
Not blocked by debris
Black mangrove water
Not dead — but sanguine
And still
with the sediment
Of centuries
Of womanthought
Dead gossamer dreams
And diamond hard as rocksand

Words scooped
From mountain streams
Cold and clean
Polished pebbles
Of loves and lies
And all
That inbetween

My words wash
In bright metallic blue
The bluemetal madness
Of my sisters' rage
Rushing through rivers
And crests
Of waterfalls
Breaking into
Storm, snaking
To the open sea
And if I am fertile now
This birth
I bring...
A birthing of
My Womanvoice, green
And glowing
And faithful to her own
Dread truth...
Mangrove diamonds
Splitting
The ascendancy dark
With crystal
Light.

Note: Mama Glo is a benign and powerful female figure in the folklore of Trinidad. Her name derives from Mama De L'Eau. She is the protector of rivers and their environment. Her appearance is a combination of woman and water-snake.

Lima Fabien

MUSE DISCRETE

Toujours la même muse
Toujours aussi cruelle
Berceau de la clarté
Berceau dans les ténèbres
Primant le beau pinson
Et la marche funèbre
Recopiant sans cesse
Le fardot de bois sec
D'un esprit en détresse
Brûlant à chaque pièce
Pour s'en aller toujours
Optant pour la détresse
Au sourire qui se fige
Chauffant les doigts sanglants
D'une eau pure et limpide
Evitant chaque aiguille
Montée sur le chassis
Débouchant sur la terre
Les rires du splendide
Eteignant la lumière
Pleurant pour chaque frère
Plongeant dans une mer
Mouillée de la misère

DISCRETE MUSE

Always the same muse
Always as cruel
Cradle of lucidity
Cradle in the shadows
Surpassing the lovely lark
And the funeral march
Copying over and over
The bundle of kindling
Of a spirit in distress
Burning in every room
To leave forever
Choosing distress
Over a fixed smile
Warming her bloody fingers

49

With a pure and limpid water
Avoiding every needle
Mounting on the stretching frame
Releasing into the world
A splendid laughter
Extinguishing light
Crying for each brother
Diving into a sea
Fed my misery

Rajandaye Ramkissoon-Chen

WHEN THE HINDU WOMAN SINGS CALYPSO

The moon takes on the glint of sun
Sleep flies, eyelids open
Legs supine rise to rhythm,
Past the midnight.

There, where she was born
In those early days
The village lamplight
With the cock's last crow
Was out. Feet huddled
Fast in sleep.

Strings of rhinestone now
'Purdah' her forehead
Her hair is frizzled
To a *'Buss-up-shot'*
The long tresses of
A long tradition
Seared in the electricity
Of the mike's cord length.

The glare of stage-lights
Takes over the backyard.
There was her training
Near standpipe and river.
That was the ground where only
Girls and women danced
To 'tassa' drummings
Of pre-nuptial celbrations

Her song resounds, her
Hips gyrate, knees bend.
Her trousers balloon
Like a rich-clad Mogul's
Their shimmer sliced
Their folds open.

Her midriff's bare
Looped white with pearls
Her body sinuous
With the dance of muscle.
She stoops as for a 'limbo' number
Head held backward from the rod-fire.
Leaves of flame
Play on her bodice.

Her voice vibrates
Past stage to audience,
Through all transmissions
The whole country listens
Night insects, they too
Stop their churrings
As she sings and 'winds'
To calypso and 'pan'
With a 'tassa' blending.

Phyllis Allfrey

THE CHILD'S RETURN

For Jean Rhys

I remember a far tall island
floating in cobalt paint
The thought of it is a childhood dream
torn by a midnight plaint

There are painted ships and rusty ships
that pass the island by,
and one dark day I'll board a boat
when I am ready to die

The timbers will creak and my heart will break
and the sailors will lay my bones
on the stiff rich grass, as sharp as spikes,
by the volcanic stones.

Nan Peacocke

ABOUT POEMS

We damage poems so easily with our own need for self-justification, our need to be forgiven, to complain, and since a poem comes to light only in your hands, there's always the urge to use it to say only what you want (which is your particular propaganda), instead of allowing your spirit to be joined by the poem in revealing the images that, because they live in all our minds and our lives, are our collective and cultural inheritance to resist the suffocating embrace of the "one true reality" as it is lived.

Poems release the images, reveal the hidden rage or love in what has happened, about what we have done, our experience as a people. Poems release the "yes" we each have chained to the dungeon wall, or that we let out only when we've dressed it appropriately that it may mix in the company of other well dressed "yesses".

Poems love to break down our constructions of the world. They set the most pitiful experiences, the most imperial forms of control to face each other as though they were equal (or reversed) in power. Poems are always rebelling against Now. That's what they do. They raise hell about how Now is unjust, uncertain. They anticipate how Now will be the next thing. And poems are eternal rebels against all social relations since these must be contractual arrangements of power which are always to the advantage of some elite and therefore causing misery in the hearts of the people (the home of poems).

Poems love causing disturbances. They are poor. They steal the gold cape of the king and run around in it like it was *everybody's*. They are considered inconsequential, but they have brought down governments (starting with the ones in our heads) and they survive not only empires but generations.

I once found an image of love as a great form hidden just under the landscape. We walk all over it not realizing where we are and that it gives the landscape its form. Suddenly we catch a glimpse of a shoulder, a great hand, what we thought was a hill, a peninsula, a river bed. Then I realized how poems are found, even when your eyes are cast downwards. And when love teaches you the courage to stand and look up, poems are high flying kites. A poem is a fierce faced kite too.

Lynette Atwell

RECLAMATION

For V.S. Naipaul

The grass that claims the verge
And forever seems to reclaim the roads
Incursions on the black tarmac
Nature claiming back her territory
That you foolishly had thought
You had won
Perpetual struggle.
Within oneself,
And outside oneself,
Claiming and reclaiming territory,
Or is it the hostile environment,
Which will claim all to itself
And leave you to bush and undergrowth
Which will reclaim you
To its sinister silence

Pauline Melville

HONOR MARIA

Honor Maria, I see you
Sitting at your typewriter
Surrounded by wild fig trees
Bound with dark green Elephants' Ears
Dry rustling Mother-in-law's tongue
Whispers ceaselessly by the stone trellis
As you tap-tap out the tale
Of Hilda Riot's battle with Mawga lion —
To which Mrs. Orange-Hat bore silent witness —
Or tap-tap out the sagas of street-vendors
Who fly, upright, through the air from Haiti
With boxes of raisins under their arms.

A dark mother, familiar with the names of plants
Birthed a daughter
Eyes green as Negril sea,
Hair blonde as the golden sea-horse
That dances upside down in the waves.
Fair Jamaica.

Honor Maria, I see you
Where the wild cane grows
Near the river at Castleton,
Or standing on that rackety bridge
By the deserted sugar mill.
But, I daresay,
You are, right now, in downtown Kingston
Up to your ankles in the garbage
That steams through gutters
After torrential rain,
Railing, with silver-bangled fist,
At the murder of your friends,
And cursing because the car won't start.

Bruised by Jamaican stones,
Deserted by Mafu
(for a Japanese reggae band)
Serenaded by seventy revolutionaries
From a neighbouring island,
You still made in tree tops
A sanctuary for the strange women artists
Of your own country.
Honor Maria, I see you
Hacking poetry from the undergrowth
Of Cockpit Country,
Pummelling plays from the shanty-town,
Snatching at the last bottle of sweet white wine
From the supermarket shelf,
Reclining, in Violet's freshly laundered skirt,
On the patchwork bedspread,
Stabbing at the paper with your angry pen.
And all the while, Stonyhill dogs bark
At phantom gunmen under the banyan tree.

Claire Harris

NO GOD WAITS ON INCENSE

For Rosemary

while babies bleed this is not the poem i wanted
it is the poem i could   though it is not that insistent
worm   it will not burrow through deaf ears
lay its eggs in your brain   yet it is all
for change
and it is not that beautiful weapon
it will not explode in the gut
despite your need   this poem is not that gift
it brings you nothing   you who insist on drinking
let your buckets into green and ruined wells   haul
in darkness   village women will lead you smiling
step back polite in the face of skulls
this poem will not catch you as you fall
not a net   no   it is nothing   this poem
not a key   not a charm   not chicken soup
and it is no use at all   at all
nothing at all
it won't beat a drum   it can't dance   it can't
even claim to be written in dust if this morning
the Bow sky-sheeted in light   the silver air is bright
with balloons   yet it talks from a dark bed
this poem   though no
woman can lie curled beneath its covers
can hide before boots
can hope to be taken for bundles of clothes   can hope
not to cry out when the knife probes
pray her blood not betray her   nor the tiny sigh
no   this poem   not even a place where anyone is safe
it can nothing   still nothing   still nothing at all
at all   in the night and disinterested air this poem
leaves no wound

ON READING ADRIENNE RICH

each night she walks a slow green tunnel
between noisy poplars to find the birth room
while the trees bulge and scramble
in a fervour of warning
their screams and curses joy and denial invoke
a path that tilts and stumbles
then she is in vague corridors and there is no one
in this enterprise she is without a guide
urgent from door to door like a drunk
in a desperate corridor pleading her way in
she asks   *is this the place*
but the doors do not open

her now blind hands touching the wood
she feels beyond those doors a place safe for
children in the glare of arc lamps
high cold tables   surgical masks   men & women
coach and coax   *you're doing great kid there's a good girl*
she stands beyond the ancient doors
knowing there is nothing for it
she must give birth to herself alone
from this knowledge she turns wildly seeking
safety she scours the dream for a place
dark cool dry sand   but the alleys
blind her turn her away from the
vast space opening inside her   from such a dream
she wakes to the chatter of house sparrows
in the kitchen she finds him
the morning smell of coffee   the newspaper rustling
drowning in the scent of her sleep
she lays her cheek on his bald head
and clings   holding herself to not
holding him to dream her dream

The Mother

Marlene Nourbese Philip

AND OVER EVERY LAND AND SEA

Meanwhile Proserpine's mother Ceres, with panic in her heart vainly sought her daughter over all lands and over all the sea.

QUESTIONS! QUESTIONS!

Where she, where she, where she
be, where she gone?
Where high and low meet I search,
find can't, way down the islands' way
I gone — south:
day-time and night-time living with she,
down by the just-down-the-way sea
she friending fish and crab with alone,
in the bay-blue morning she does wake
with kiskeedee and crow-cock —
skin green like lime, hair indigo-blue,
eyes hot like sunshine-time;
grief gone mad with crazy — so them say.
Before questions too late,
before I forget how they stay,
crazy or no crazy I must find she.

It would take a long time to name the lands and seas over which the goddess wandered. She searched the whole world — in vain.....

CLUES

She gone — gone to where and don't know
looking for me looking for she;
is pinch somebody pinch and tell me,
up where north marry cold I could find she —
Stateside, England, Canada — somewhere about,
"she still looking for you —
try the Black Bottom — Bathurst above Bloor,
Oakwood and Eglinton — even the suburbs them,
but don't look for indigo hair and
skin of lime at Ontario Place,
or even the reggae shops;

stop looking for don't see and can't —
you bind she up tight tight with hope,
she own and yours knot up in together;
although she tight with nowhere and gone
she going find you, if you keep looking."

....the earth opened up a way for me and, after passing deep down
through its lowest caverns, I lifted up my head again in these regions,
and saw the stars which had grown strange to me.

DREAM-SKINS

dream-skins dream the dreaming:
(in two languages)
Sea-shell

> low low over the hills
> > she flying
> up up from the green of sea
> she rise emerald
> > skin
> > fish belt
> weed of sea crown she

Feather-skin

> lizard-headed
> i suckle her
> suckling me
> > flat
> thin like the
> > host
> round and white
> > she swells enormous with
> milk and child

Sea-lace

> in one hand the sun
> the moon in the other
> round and round
> she swing them from chains
> let fly till they come
> to the horizon
> of rest

Blood-cloth

      wide wide
      i open my mouth
           to call

      the blood-rush come up
           finish
      write she name
      in the up-above sky
      with some clean white rag
      she band up my mouth
           nice nice

Blood-cloths
(dream in a different language)

    sand
      silence
        desert
          sun
    the wide of open mouth
    blood of rush
    hieroglyphs
    her red
    inscriptions
    her name
    up-above sky
        sudden
    clean of white
        cloths
      wounded mouth
    broad back
        hers
    to tie
      carry
      bear

Ceres knew it (Proserpine's girdle) well, and as soon as she recognized it, tore her dishevelled hair, as if she had only then learned of her loss: again and again she beat her breast.

SIGHTINGS

Nose to ground — on all fours — I did once
smell that smell,
on a day of once —
upon a time, tropic with blue
when the new, newer and newest of leaves compete,
in the season of suspicion she passed,
then and ago trailed the wet and lost of smell;
was it a trompe d'oeil —
the voice of her sound, or didn't I once
see her song, hear her image call
me by name — my name — another sound, a song,
the name of me we knew she named
the sound of song sung long past time,
as I cracked from her shell —
the surf of surge
the song of birth.

*All opening quotations are from Ovid's Metamorphoses
(transl. Mary M. Innes).*

R.H. Douglas

AN' YOU WILLING TO DO IT AGAIN!

Don't tell me,
Yes, I know
Soon you forget
all the pain,
agony and sweat
an' you willing to
do it again.

Fifteen times you uterus
stretch
'til its elasticity
run out
an' you nearly bleed
to death
Fifteen children just
ain't enough
an' you willing to
do it again!

Three caesarean sections
ain't that enough!?
'cause he want
more children
three just ain't enough
an' you willing to
do it again!

"Ah Father help me
get over this one,
an' I never spreading
my legs
for no man again...."
that plea upon
the delivery bed
You soon forget
once the onslaught
of pain subside,
an' you willing to
do it again!

Arnoldine M. Burgos

Ben leven ontwaakt
diep in mij
ik ben bang
leven
geen leven
angst voor de toekomst
mijn toekomst
haar toekomst
abortus
een recht van elke vrouw.

A life wakes up
Deep inside of me
I am afraid
Life
No Life
Fear for the future
My future
Her future
Abortus
A right of every woman

Olive Senior

THE MOTHER

Muma mi belly soon
grow bed so small
last night Uncle Paul
bizniz with me
didn't know till he done —

Hush yu mout little gal
have no right
talk such nonsense
how come yu so shurance
and force ripe. Uncle Paul
help with school fees
and dress say he like

— what go on
under cover

girls look nice when they go
off to school

Muma no school today
mi body a hot me. Mi
head dis a grow muma
beg yu no lash me

One night you even say
yu own father did try
o god pickney nowadays
so wicked and lie
Study books dem not story.
If you get heddication dont
have to be like me

As for that lazy bitch there the
one Mistress Marshall she going
get her comeuppance as soon as a done

she think I dont know when she
think I round back who she entertain
round front say is insurance they selling
dont know where she gone in her
prison-pon-wheel. Say I tief out
the rice. Say black people not nice

Who dont know it will feel.

And where Bobby eh? A just know seh is trouble
that boy done get into. Do nutten but walk
street keep company. Toyota have no right
pull up door at night call the boy out say is
business he gone on. What right boy that age
have with business and firearm (that he swear he
dont have).

O God but this town is a crosses.

Michelle Cliff

THE LAND OF LOOK BEHIND

*On the edge of each canefield or "piece" was a watch house, a tiny
structure with one entry. These were used for the babies of nursing
slaves who worked in the fields. An older woman was in charge of the
infants and the mothers came there for feeding time.*
                    tourist brochure of the Whim Great House

A tiny structure with one entry
walls guttered with mortar
molasses   coral   sand
hold the whole thing fast.

One hundred years later
the cut limestone
sunned and salted
looks like new.

And feels like? And feels like?
I don't know.
Describe it.
Sad? Lost? Angry?
Let me get my bearings.

Outside
A tamarind tree with a dead nest in the first crotch
Dense mud construction
Immense. The inhabitants long gone.
Hard brown pods crack underfoot
The soursweet flesh is dried.
Inedible.

Inside
One thin bench faces a blank wall.
No message from the watchwomen here.
No HELP ME carved in the mortar or the stone.
Try to capture the range —

What did their voices sound like?
What tongues? What words for day and night?
Hunger? Milk?
What songs devised to ease them?

Was there time to speak? To sing?
To the riverain goddesses
The mermaids bringing secrets
To bring down Shango's wrath.

No fatting-houses here.
Nowhere to learn the secrets
except through some new code
in spaces they will never own.

How many voices? How many drops of milk?
How many gums daubed with rum to soothe the teething
or bring on sleep?

How many breasts bore scars?
Not the sacred marking of the Carib —
but the mundane mark of the beast.

How many dropped in the field?
How many bare footfalls across the sand floor?
How many were buried?
I leave through the opening and take myself home.

Note: Shango is the Yoruban god of thunder, lightning and vengeance.

Afua Cooper

MY MOTHER

My mother planted fields
married a man
bore ten children
and still found time
to have her own business
I remember once
she and I
were going to work
the plot of land
she rented from someone
we heard the missionary's car
coming down the road

she jumped over a culvert to hide
because she had on a pair
of my father's pants
the church disapproved of women
wearing men's clothing
when the sun was steadily going westward
we hurried from the field
she had to rush home
to cook the family's meal
she seemed able to do anything
and i think that in one
of her past lives
she was a leader of some sort

my mother planted fields
married a man
bore ten children
and still found time
to run her own business

Audrey Ingram-Roberts

GIRL-CHILD, LOVE-CHILD

Do you think because you were easily made
that I don't love you?
Do you think because your father and I fell
lazily into each others arms that rainy Sunday
when Nat King Cole crooned and the saucy cat
Pollyanna sat in the window swishing her tail
and watching through oriental eyes of pretended
disapproval and veiled curiosity, that we abhor you?
You'd better understand me girl that I won't let
you waste you.
You'd better hear me girl that I do love you,
fiercely love you.

Nora E. Peacocke

DEMETER

Once there was a little lady
Her eyes were brown and very bright
To others she was just a baby
But to me she brought the world
more light

PLATANAL LULLABY

Go to sleep! Go to sleep my dear,
Safe within the Sandman's care.
He will gently take your hand,
Lead you to a happy land.

There you'll dream, dream of bottled milk,
And of puppies dressed in coat of silk.
You shall also see goats of pedigree,
And a cocker-doodle-do who won't crow to startle you.

Donkeys grey, chicks in fine array,
All in grand parade by the Sandman made.
Rattles, teddy bears, bunnies with long ears,
The kind Sandman will show to babes who with him go.

Flags and gay balloons, sun and stars and moon,
Endless things to suck, only dreams can bring such luck.
Do not fight, surrender to his might,
In the Sandman's arms share those dreamland charms.

Cease your peevish cries,
Close your little eyes.
The Sandman knows what's best,
Babies must have rest.

Go to sleep! Go to sleep my dear,
Safe within the Sandman's care.
He will gently take your hand,
Lead you to a happy land.

Leone Ross

SHE IS

She is...
She is...
    A blanket—stifling and constricting—a blanket whose
    security
    I love yet hate—a blanket which holds me too close—
    too warm.
She is...
She is...
    a tornado-ripping apart my foundations
    and crushing me into miniscule bits of shame...
    yet after the
    tornado comes the rain of her tears, my tears...
    mingling till
    we forget our sorrow and laugh
            once again.
She is...
She is...
        a cat. A black panther, sleek and beautiful —
            A tiger..waiting for its prey...
        A kitten playing with a ball of wool...
            a lioness, majestic and aloof.
She is...
    a guardian, a friend, a confidante,
    an enemy, one loved with a love as strong as her own
    will.
    She is good yet bad...black yet white...happy yet sad..
    ..a kaleidoscope of emotions and colours and moods.
She is...
    My mother.

Grace Nichols

PRAISE SONG FOR MY MOTHER

You were
water to me
deep and bold and fathoming
You were
moon's eye to me
pull and grained and mantling

You were
sunrise to me
rise and warm and streaming

You were
the fishes red gill to me
the flame tree's spread to me
the crab's leg/the fried plantain smell
                                    replenishing replenishing
Go to your wide futures, you said

Elaine Savory

BIRTH POEM

i

when you have
given
birth
(whatever that means)

it figures less as an idea

ii

it is giving
myself
to birth

i found too difficult

iii

crisis of maleness
is in the same order as betrayals
which made me fear
to birth

iv

we refuse to be part of cycles
& earth will plough us back harder
for the next crop

v

creating
requires
the perfect balance
between shell & centre
come to that ripeness
which destroys

vi

birth is a dissolution
which begins
& you are never
separate
again
afterwards

Lydia Geerman

MITA...MUCHA...MAMA

Bida sa tin buelta!
Doita, bisiña di tur hende
konosi pa su trabou
a sa di lanta
su pret'i wowo, Mita
néchi, firme, du respet.
Tin bes dams su kara
tribí di hubentut
otro dia un sonrisa suave
k'un konose soberbia, ta dorné.

Ketu, ketu, Mita' kana trese
un leli blanko, puro, tenchi
pa su mai yudé kuidé.
Flor di Mita' sali boltu
sin sumpiña ni tronkon
hana chens di pega drechi
mucho delikado pa lidia yu su so.

Rayo di solo a sigui hasi mofa
dje sombra di su bida.
Ni luna ni strea por a penetra
e skuridat di su tristesa.
Su futuro di splendor
a para, bira duro, dof, pisá.
Djo lag'e kriatura pronto
debolbé legria i sperensa
pa hunto nan por krusa mondi
piki anglo, weta blenchi chupa flor.

Kada bes mi mira yuchi
bebe pechu di su mami-mucha
manera un naño ta hender mi sintí
pakiko net é?
Shimaron en' ser kriá
sabiduria n' falté.
O kisas e balansa di
amor, atenshon i guia
kos, ehèmpel i konseho
tog no tabata poni
n'e bon midí?

MITA...CHILD...MOTHER

Life does have her turns
Doita, everybody's neighbour
known for her hardworking nature,
saw right to raise
her apple of the eye, Mita
nice, firm and dutiful.
Sometimes the little lady's face
audacious with young blood
other times a soft smile
without impertinence, adorned it.

Quietly Mita brought
a white, pure, delicate lily
for her mother to help
her taking care of it.
Mita's flower sprang into existence
without thorns nor stems
getting a chance to become firm,
too delicate to look after a child all by herself.

Sunrays continued to sneer at
the shadow of her life.
Neither the moon nor the stars
could penetrate the darkness of her sorrow.
Her splendid future
stood still, hardened, grey and heavy.
Let's hope the baby soon
will return her joy and hope
so together they'll be able to cross fields
picking flowers, looking at humming-birds sucking honey.

Everytime I see the baby
sucking the breast of her child-mother
a prickle hinders my conscience
why she?
She wasn't raised in ignorance
knowledge wasn't witheld from her.
Or maybe the balance of
love, attention and guidance,
things, example and counseling
however were not handed to her
in the right proportion?

Rosanne Brunton

SEE DE DOOR

My sister ask me
So old you getting
When I eating a piece of cake from you
I tell her
Not me child
Nobody going to tell my children
See de door

Five children I have
Each one a different father
But all is mine
Like the fingers of my hand
Dont tell me you dont like this one
Because I tell you
See de door

You cant like me
And dont like the child
You say you dont like to sit at the table with no child
I say, I teach them the table
If you dont like it
See de door
You say you going
I dont tie up nobody foot
Leave the child here
I will work
And I will mind it
Whenever you ready
See de door

Now all of them get big
One in London
One in America
I stay three, six, nine months
I forget my teeth on the bed home
But I get accustom
Not one child tell me
See de door

Marina Ama Omowale Maxwell

FOR WOMEN GOING UNDER

For Malachi, the mother who burnt herself in Trinidad.
And for all the others.

Deep brown moths
flit in and out
battering our spirits
with edged wings.
Beating our nakedness
Flapping against
the shutters
and the stones
of the "desperate silences" of it all.

Ah, that you would just come quietly, Sister Death
Take us silently —
so we do not go down in flames
cave in
walk under buses
drown in pills
or be strangled.

So that our children will not blame us
And our past husbands
in more pain
resent again
that we take our lives
into our own hands
Forgive me Mother.

Creep up/silently
over the walls

we build meticulously every night
Spare us — the continuous agonies.

Madeline Coopsammy

FOR MY DAUGHTER

Cradling your soft cheek
I think about the poets
who have enshrined
their immortal daughters
within their lyric lines
and know that neither mother love
nor mother prayers
will ever stay the drift of tides
or thwart the hurricane or blizzard
from its ordained path
that though today we wrest
with punctuation
and with
the wonderment of numbers
the cycle has begun
and though I strive to hold you
from the untoward
hands of fate
perhaps you too
will one day turn from me
as I have turned from her
the one who bore me
and that someday
as she, my mother sits and waits
in her heat-encrusted cocoon
waiting for the evening
and the cooling Trades
to bring release from day's
too wearisome round
catching the dying moments of life's short
joys
will I too, wait
safe in my Prairie cocoon
while my daughter
treads her life within Manhattan's dizzy mazes
or rides the surf in California sun
and I, despairing and disheartened
assail the Heavens with my prayers
as now she does for me?
as she has done
through nights when she, unknown to me

was ever watching
as I battered on the Shakespeare texts
unfurled the mysteries of conjugations and declensions
and she, not knowing what I had to know
yet waiting, always waiting
was there to fill the cocoa cups
to mend and starch virginal blouses
and the fading Convent tunics
and all the while believing
that one day I, the favoured daughter
would bring an honour to her house
which honour yet is still to come
but for her patience and her faith
I can only ask, for you, my own
the honour I have yet   to find.

Ruth Sawh

NERVES

I wish I had nerves like
        spaghetti
I'd stretch them long
Pull them thin
Wind them 'round
Twist them
Jag them
Jolt them
Cut them
Eat them
So that maybe
I'd have more to go around

Nydia Ecury

KANTIKA PA MAMA TERA

Mama, Tera, k'a parimi,
Hesú bo yu su alma
tin di krusa
un desierto largu
anto desolá
su so.

Ya mi no ta riska
ni di buska
un alivio pa mi pena;
ku bálsamo kisas
di un soño tur bruhá
òf den promesanan
ku ta bai i bin'
ku bientu...

Ma at'awé
mi yu chiki
a karisiá mi kurason
ku un kantika dushi
k'el a kanta
pa mi so.

Ta pesei, Mama Tera,
mi ta baha
mi kabes kansá
pa mi sunchi
bo matris gastá.

Si den tal akto
di revernsia
na mi kara
bo por topa
un lágrima ta dual,
Mama Tera,
pa bo e ta,
mi regalo di gratitut,
pasobra:
Mama mi tambe ta!

SONG FOR MOTHER EARTH

In dwelling on your face,
Old Mother Earth,
my soul must cross
a desert vast
and desolate
alone.

I do not even dare
to soothe my pain
with the comfort
of a dream
or a promise
in the wind.

And yet,
I bow my tired head
to kiss
your weary womb
because
I am a Mother, too.

If in this act
of reverence
should you detect
upon my face
a wandering tear,
it is for you,
Dear Mother Earth,
my gift
of gratitude
because today
my son has sung
a song
to me.

Ramabai Espinet

FOR GRACE MY MOTHER

You moved through agonies of old lace
And silver antiquities
Made you burn
With loyalties
Of rock and water
Unburdening never.

Phyllis Allfrey

THE GIPSY TO HER BABY

For Phina

Oh flower of my flesh, whose blossoming
Brought me wild pain and even wilder joy,
Immortally delightful baby thing,
Less than an angel, greater than a toy:
Out of my body's darkness rudely torn
To navigate the ocean of the world
That men might boast — *another babe is born,*
Another flag of challenge is unfurled!

How you will roam, and whither, who can guess?
All that I give you is a heritage
Of bold adventuring and loveliness,
Of merriment, and wisdom amply sage;
Take these few weapons in your tiny hands
And sally forth to meet a crouching fate.
Bless with your darling presence many lands:
Bless with your love your heart's true intimate.

The Lover

Margaret D. Gill

I WANT TO MAKE YOU CRY TONIGHT

I want to make you
   cry tonight
I want to shake you
  and break you
       and take you apart and then —
Want to create you
         tonight

To begin you
And sing you
And bring you
    to
  where
(if you care to)
They say heaven is
     heaven is
     heaven is.

I want to make you
   cry tonight
Like a big ole man child.
Shall I liberate you from all that holding in and
               holding on and
               self sufficient?
— I may not succeed now! But
I shall certainly try —
      cry
    cry, cry
      cry (it's good for you).

POEM FOR DONNA

Did I begin too soon?
Were you waiting
in the wings and wishing
that we'd take
the Second Act
a bit more slow?

> I'd tired of the carousel
> that music sound, too much
> too much like "London Bridge"
> and "falling down", and humpty dumpty
> leaving all of his mess
> for me to clean again
> I had become a tenor pan —
> this carnival could not begin
> with violins.

Was my wining too rude?
Could have arranged
my smile, just so,
my dance, my breasts
your children and
your coffee cups —
itó piccolo, or demitasse
or anything you'd want. Ta raso!
for cups too small to hold
the carnival I bring,
no longer serve my soul!

Was my music too loud!
or (Oh, the thought, the thought!)
You like some other play play man
thinking carnival was not serious
or women could not be ole' mas

> God I thought you understood —
> ......you offered J'ouvert Morning
> Why now and suddenly
> Ashwednesday

Audrey Ingram-Roberts

CRICKET, US AND OTHER GAMES

But then again I'd been tooting,
rooting up a racket of applause
for me when I knew you were not
listening; so now I could shout, foul!
Play, rain stops play, tea break.
A chance to take a look at the game
from behind the wicket of pretended freedom.
You'd fielded my catch enough now
to snap the latch and show, foul!
But then again you'd not been watching
to see me reach across and balm your pain.

And then again I'd not been smelling
the eucalyptus bandages you soothed
on my raw hurt.
Play, good play day sun day.
Play me love, skills away, play
for the fun of it, for the hell of it.
And then again, we may be listening,
visions enlightened behind striped bars
of perceived jail, for accepting each other,
unconditionally.

OLD ROMANCE

I watch them many a Sunday at the beach.
He perhaps 67 and she, 65, maybe.
Sunbathers of a peculiar brand.
She more sprightly, helps him to his feet
and waves him on to take a dip.

No Coppertone, Jourdan shades or Cardin
blankets attend them, nor even jaded dogs
nor rowdy children to frolic in the sand.
But from their baskets they pull pots of
scented peas and rice, shallow dishes of
vermilion edged plantains, sweating bowls
of crisp chicken or beige cracked conch.

Theirs is a ritual feast in loving friendship.
Each Sunday I smile at this old romance.

giannina elena rijsdijk

TWO POEMS FOR I.F.D.

1.

No
Mi no man tai yu
I no de in' katibo
I fri
Yu kan waka go
pe you wani
M'abi wan begi nomo
Drai kon na mi.

2.

But when I don't feel him
around me anymore
I feel my soul
flow out of me
like liquid ice
So cold, so cold.

AUGUST 25, 1986

God rest your soul, my dear
Goodbye
You could have been
my brother, lover, friend.
But you were a soldier
And soldiers.......
they are bound to die

Woman
Just shed your tears
I too, would cry
But then
didn't you know
Your husband was a soldier
You became a widow long ago
That day you saw him
clad in green.

Arnoldine M. Burgos

POEM I

Als een vonk
die steecls weer aun het brandende
beo faja ouwr ontsnapt
klein en toch vel brandend
vol van energie
is de liefde die in my
ontwaakt voor jou

POEM I

Like a spark
scaping from the fire brand
small but severe burning
full of energy
is the love awaiting in
me for you

POEM II

myn liefde voor jou
is als een oliebrand
die eenmaal outvlamt
blyft branden
door windstolen aangeset
tot een met te beteugelen felheid
en by regen
bescheiden maar toch brandend

POEM II

my love for you
is like an oilfire
which once flames
keeps on burning
set to an irresistible
severity by wind
and rain
small but still burning

Triveni Rahim

DIALECSTASY

Massaging your body with my fingertips;
An ecstasy of sensation — for you, for me...
Your shoulders, bottom, feet respond to my touch,
Arching up to meet my hands, breasts, legs.
Time and place stand still as our nerve-endings leap
anemone-like toward each other;
Electrical impulses bridging the ganglia of our separateness.

Drinking our saliva, sweat, tears;
Your tongue exploring my vulva, wooing my own secretions;
Semen in my mouth becomes yours again in a kiss;
My menstrual blood you suck — and return to my breasts,
mouth, face.
We create a heady chemistry of body fluids and heat
Made by blood and muscle and nerves.

Eyes shut, blocking out vision;
Ears fine-tuned to the music
of our breathing, heartbeat and moans;
You lying on top of me, behind me, beside me, around me,
Your penis a snake penetrating this elemental woman
In a wave-like rhythm of movement;
Dialectical — at once motionless and propelling —
Towards a synthesis of being.

Words have always been important to me; they give me a sense
of power, control.
As if once defined, analysed, a thing is mine.
Your sensuousness challenges both the rational and the
possessive,
Expressing meaning through a touch, a look, a hug — to me, to
other women.
When I described my father's indentureship and his mother's
suffering you simply held me...
Healing my bleeding wounds of race, of class, of gender.

Meiling Jin

LOVERS

Cry, for the death of something in us
Let's say innocence,
When we loved without knowledge
Of each other.
When to each other
We unveiled
The hidden parts of ourselves,
We both stood back
In horror and disbelief.

Leleti Tamu

CASSELBERRY HARVEST

We embraced and your arms
slipped slowly around me like
the limbs and branches of the
casselberry tree,
that grows from the dark moist
earth of ashanti soil

Your locks brown and delicious
carries the fragrance from the
blossoms of that tree

In the language of our
foremothers, casselberry must
mean sun kissed days, blanketing
a soft orchard, with the
indigo sweetness of you

I anticipate the familiar
flavour of your casselberry
harvest.

Mahadai Das

DIAMOND

Long lost in their laughing tale
of blue Caribbean waters
or Arizona nightskies; entranced,
a sleepwalker in a privileged
vision, I am bedazzled yet
by those blue-diamond eyes.

A mysterious woman flew
from Europe's winter,
with you strapped to her arm
like a late Christmas parcel.
A diamond shone on her finger
like light.
Held securely,
you were marked out by her mark,
she by yours.

Everywhere, in whatever manner
you go, you must wear her sign
like a banner. Alright, medieval
knight. Exhibit your trophy
from the Holy Crusades. Bear
your cross, a hand against the breast.
Pledge devotion to your Christian sect!

Though a cross drove a wedge
between you and my heart, I wear
a blue diamond spawned from your eyes.
Love's dumb grief wreathes my lips
as I turn my hand, examining
its ghostly gleam in the moonlight.

Amryl Johnson

GIFTS

Is so long she ehn see de man
man ehn come tuh see she in so long
He was comin' by she every day
every day every day
bringin' she flowers an presents
presents an' ting
he in dey wit' she fuh hours
hours he in dey wit' she
Wen we see she nex' she smilin'
smilin' like she do somethin' clever
Dat was long pas' look she now
now look wha' happen tuh she

De man stop callin' so long
so long he ehn come see she
Look how she belly big
big like it goin' to buss
An' de girl lookin' so proud
proud before dey does fall
De girl lookin' in we face an' smilin'
smilin' like she so somethin' special
Like she feel she do somethin clever
Clever? any fool can make baby
So ah hah tuh ask she
she should be hangin' she head in shame
Mavis, wha' de arse yuh hah tuh smile 'bout?
'bout time she start showin' shame
Miss Ross, yuh too dry up tuh know
'bout love
Love? Wha' she know 'bout it sheself?
Dis chile is de bes' gift ah could have
have a bit ah shame ah say
We love child is de bes' gift he could leave
leave? we KNOW he did leave!
You wouldn't understan' 'bout such tings, Miss
    Ross
Miss Ross you shoulda box she mout'
An' de girl stroke she belly an' smile
smile should be on de other side ah she face
Nuttin' ah tell she could change she mind
she mind ehn workin' too good
She say she happy as she is
is love some ah dem does call it,
    Miss Ross is Love

Joy Wilson-Tucker

QUESTIONS

Am I to believe
That you expect me to
Live each day without
Caring for the needs of another?
That because I care you will
No longer trust my feelings?

Am I to believe that life must
Exist only with you?
That there is no other time or place
To find comfort?
Should I cease to search for knowledge
Understanding — kindness, because you
Feel you can fulfill all my needs?
If we were mutually helping each other,
Would I feel as I do distant
Unfulfilled?
And as long as these questions remain,
What will become of me?
As I — seek the answers
To goals — unreached — desires unfulfilled,
Must I stifle my life
While I await the answers
To — These Questions?

Margaret Watts

WHITHER THOU GOEST

Both in black, the gray one's hollow eyes
hover over a mouth stretched tight round
dogged words. Ruth's eyes resonate,
tempered by brown gentle hair, attuned
to an easy smile. Both of them hold the basket —
Ruth's harvested barley;

                         Ruth alone carries the seed,
sown in her body, sold for the breeding of Israel —
a mother-in-law's word obeyed by the mother of Obed.

The red sun in the orange sky
mocks the colourless refrain:
    Whither Thou goest, I will go
    Thy people shall be my people.

We shy from the vivid hues,
accept Naomi's dark design,
resign ourselves to lie with a man,
insure his line, people the world
with singing Davids who propagate the faith.

Asha Radjkoemar

POEM

je baadde
naast de put

onze ogen

de geur
van de bedompte
stal
het stampen
van hoeven

sterren
die door de gaten
van de zinkplaten
druppelden

dan
je zucht
toen je
klaar
met me was

POEM

you were bathing
next to the well
our eyes

the smell
of the stuffy
stable
the stamping
of hooves

stars
that trickled
through the holes
of the galvanised sheets

then

your sigh
when you
had done
with me

Aimée Eloidin

SI J'ÉTAIS EUTERPE...

Si j'étais Euterpe,
Chaque soir, au clair de lune,
A l'aide de ma lyre,
Je te conduirais au palais de Morphée.
Tandis qu'une sirene à la voix mélodieuse
Bercerait ton sommeil,
Mes doigts caresseraient
Ta toison couleur miel.

Mais je ne suis que Melpomène
Qui fait naître sur son passage
Le drame, les cris et les larmes!

Serais-tu Celui qui changerait me vie?
Serais-tu Adonis ou mieux encore Phoebus?
Oui, tu l'es, je le sais, car chaque fois que tu passes
Je me sens devenir, gaie, enjouée, volubile:
Melpomène cède alors son royaume à Thalie.

IF I WERE EUTHERPE...

If I were Eutherpe
Each evening, by moonlight,
With the aid of my lyre
I would take you to Morpheus' palace,
While a siren's melodious voice
Rocked you to a slumber,
My fingers would caress
Your honey-coloured fleece.
But I am only Melpomene
In whose passage springs up
great drama, shouting and tears!

Will you be the one to change my life?
Will you be my Adonis or better still Phoebus?
Yes, you are, I know it, for each time you come by,
I become talkative, happy, full of joy:
And Melpomene gives over her realm to Thalia.

POEM

J'ai peur des couples qui
s'enlacent, s'embrassent,
se bécotent, se tripotent,
sous le regard gêné ou attendri
des voyeurs involontaires.
J'ai peur des couples qui
à tout bout de champs,
s'appellent: chéri, chérie,
se lèchent, se pourlèchent,
se font d'interminables mamours,
sous le regard gêné ou attendri
des témoins involontaires.
Ces couples d'infidèles,
Ces couples de menteurs,
Ces couples d'hypocrites,
Ces couples de théâtre,
Couples de Carnaval!
Je préfère les couples qui
s'enlacent, s'embrassent, se
bécotent, se tripotent, se
lèchent, se pourlèchent,
se dévorent,
sous l'oeil decret de leurs quatre murs.

POEM

I'm afraid of those couples who
hug and kiss one another,
peck and paw one another,
under the discomfited look or tender gaze
of involuntary voyeurs.
I'm afraid of those couples who
at the drop of a hat,
call out darling, my sweet,
lick their lips, and each others',
whisper unending sweet nothings,
under the discomfited look or tender gaze
of involuntary witnesses.
Those couples of cheaters
Those couples of liars
Those couples of hypocrites
Those couples of actors
Carnival couples!

I prefer those couples who
hug and kiss one another
peck and paw one another
lick their lips and each others',
devour one another
under the discrete gaze of their four walls.

Afua Cooper

SIX O'CLOCK

I.

he is having supper with his family
you can hear the children's voices
his voice, her voice quieting them
he plays the role of the devoted father
                and husband
you cannot interrupt this family ritual
"i'll call you back," he says on the other end of the line

II.

you are jealous of his wife and children
for the time he spends with them
while he sees you only at intermissions

III.

you berate yourself
call yourself a fool
want to put a stop to this, make an exit
but your flesh refuses to see what your mind sees clearly

IV.

now he has stopped calling
yet his silence speaks

V.

you fight to break out of the windowless
room he has locked you in
somewhere in the tropics

Priscilla Brown

EL AMOR

El amor estuvo aquí,
era tan exquisito,
tan tierno, tan dulce.
Así es el amor.

Que lindo es el amor,
con passión, con ternura, con amor.
De ser amada, abrasada, con el amor.
De sentir el calor,
De amar sin temor,
De sentirse amado por alguien,
De ahorar el amor.

Sueño con el amor,
el bien que me hará,
a mi corazón y a mi mente,
a mi vida entera.
Solo pienso en el amor.
Qué lindo.

Quel que encuentra el amor,
recuerda éstas lineas
ahora el amor,
el amor vale mucho.
No es cada diá que, uno encuentra el amor.
Busca tu amor.
La vida necessita el amor.

LOVE

Love was here,
it was so exquisite,
so tender, so sweet.
That's how love is.

How pretty is love
with passion, with tenderness, with love.
Being loved, burned, by love.
Feeling the heat
Loving without fear
Feeling loved by someone,
Saving love.

I dream of love,
the good it will do me,
for my heart and mind,
my whole life.
I only think of love.
How pretty.

Whoever finds love
should remember these lines
now love
love is worth a lot.
You do not find love every day.

Find your love.
Life needs love.

Marina Ama Omowale Maxwell

TO MY LOVE, STILL

*In our search for Liberation we must not forget that the aim is still to
find love, between man and woman, for children, for country — to
build relationships between us of meaning and equality.*

A tree is rooted in me
and you have planted the seed.
Rooted
in my muladra chakra
it grows
and even you
cannot remove it.

Leaves will come out of my ears, green
May choke my breath
of flowers
may come
out of my mouth, poui yellow.
Around my heart
birdsongs
have built a nest
canny and warm.
Will you root my feet
with strong tendrils
or plait my entrails
in contortion?
But
there is something I have to say about it
Now.
Today — I am grown strong/er now
I can cut it down
Trim your tentacles
Bonsai your arms
concentrate your foliage
Help us grow blossoms —
No longer subject
or Object
But Gardener.
But I need your help.

Dorothy Wong Loi Sing

HET MONSTER MAN

Als kind al werd mij ingestampt
wees bang voor het monster man
Dus als ik jou eens tegen kwam
ging ik gauw aan de kant
Ik durfde niet naar jou te kijken
een witte aap, een zwarte pad
een gele slang, een bruine rat
een weerzinwekkend angstaanjagend
vormeloos gevaar
En al liep je honderd malen
mij achterna
in een poging tot kontakt
je riep je naam,
je riep je wens tot vriendschap
Ik liep honderdmalen gauw van jou vandaan
En als ik dan mijn eigen vaden zag
mijn breers mijn ooms mijn opa
bekroop mij toch de twijfel
als mannen dan te vrezen zijn
als mannen dan te mijden zijn
als mannen dan lelijk en monsters zijn
waarom heeft mijn eigen moeder
dan zelf een man?
waarom heeft mijn moeder
dan een vader?
waarom heeft mijn oma dan
een opa om zich heen?

En in mijn dromen
befon jij ta komen
en bleef ik staan
om je aan ta horen
om schuw te zien
of jij zo'n engerd was
En wat mama geleerd had
schoof ik nu aan de kant
ik keek je in de ogen
ik opende mijn hart
en liet jou erin
Ze habben mij elecht voorgelicht
je habt geen lelikj, maar een lief
gezicht
met kuiltjes

THE GENDER MONSTER-MALE

When I was just a little child
they warned me: 'For the monster-male, beware!'
So, whenever you crossed my path
I stepped aside, quickly.
I didn't dare to look you in the face:
a white gorilla, a black toad,
a yellow snake, a brown rat
an aversion-provoking fear-vibrating
formless abomination
signing 'Danger'

And even if you followed me
a hundred times
trying to reach out
in contact
You cried your name out loud,
you cried out your wish for friendship

I ran away as many a hundred times

And somethimes when I looked
at my own father
my brothers my uncles my granddad
then I started to ask myself
doubtful questions

if the male gender is to be feared
if the male gender is to be shunned
if the male gender is ugly and a monster-man
why then my own mother
has a husband?
when then my own mother
has a father?
why then my grandma has a granddad
by her side

And in my dreams
you came nearer
and I ran slower
and finally I stopped
to listen to your voice
to look shyly
if you really were so ugly
And what mama had taught me
I put aside —
I looked you in the eyes
I opened up my heart
and let you inside

They have given me wrong advice:
You are not ugly at all
You have a friendly, lovable face
with dimples in your cheeks and chin!

Charmaine Gill

LOVE-ME-NOT

Love-me-not
I tell you that I'm in love with you,
You tell me that I'm not.
You say that I love you.
And I agree.
There is a difference.
Either way, I lose.
I put the gun in my mouth,
And you pull the trigger.

PAUL

Well, isn't life just saccharine sweet:
I met you at a superficial party
Where pseudo-intellectuals,
Ourselves excluded,
Drank wine,
Ate cheese and crackers,
And talked.
You admired me because
I had the wisdom
And strength to counter-attack.

The next time I saw you,
You were in your element,
Weeping,
Crying radically,
"Art is sweat and blood and practice." and
"Culture in our reality is dead."
You stood on your soapbox,
And strutted your stuff.

I know where you are coming from
And I can laugh.
I cry because
Saccharine has a bitter after taste
And causes cancer.

Stacy Johnson

FIRST LOVE

It is so hard to bear, I stand there waiting till eternity for
you to even sway your vision,
for you to see me as the woman I am and not the girl you
perceive me to be.
Don't you think that I can feel love? Do you think that
because I am young I don't know?
Well I do know! I know the anguish of unrequited love,
the hurt and the pain,
I know what I want, I want for you to tell me that you
love me, straight from your heart.

But then I also know I'm dreaming. You're far too old for me,
I know that,
then why do I feel the way that I do? I am so confused, maybe
it's just an infatuation,
but so strong is the flame I carry for you that I know it could
not be so.
So fiercely have I been branded by this indispensable obsession
to have your love.
I know I should stop, deny my thoughts, forget my feelings,
but I can't
and I'm scared, scared because I don't want to be scorched by
the flame!

Jane King Hippolyte

MY CURSE

This is my curse
It is a married lady's curse.
It is a curse against those
Who unsex us
By enchilding us
By enmothering us
By empedestalling us
By envirgining us
And then flaunt their whores in our faces.

Against those who dark-caped
Hollow fanged
Drain us
Swearing they want us pale
And then praise the warm cheeks of their new loves
As we languish in their pallor.

I am not yet good at cursing.
Love is what I had been practising.

V.M. Albert

STICK WITH ME

(i'll make it worth your while)

Stick with me, I'll make it worth your while
I'll love you till the end, we'll be one forever
Be my lover, my friend, my all
Life and love is not worth it without you

Stay with me
You're unique, you're special, you're incredible
I've never met anyone quite like you
I don't know what I'd do without you, your love
Let's get married, one day, some day, in the future
Love me, have me, stay with me today and always.

Stay with me
She's just a friend
She means nothing to me
She's no match, you're a woman, she's just a child

Stay with me, she's not that bad
Yes I've been seeing her
Yes I've been sleeping with her
Yes I feel strongly for her
You should have known it would happen
You should have seen it coming
But for you what I feel can't ever change
Won't ever change

Stay with me
I don't know what I feel for you anymore
I don't know how it happened
But I know that I love her

Stay with me
Yes she loves me
It's been some 5 years now
Oh I did not mean to hurt you
But she's young, she's attractive, and well spoken
Yes I know, you're so special
Believe me..., I'm closer to you than you think

Stay with me I'll make it up to you
I'll make it worth your while
So what? does it matter that she is my wife?
You know I think of you a lot...
I know that she and I are one for always, forever...
But that's the way it is, fate did that to me
It was during my vision quest...
Oh but I think I love her, I just don't know
Oh please understand I did not mean to hurt you
I love you, but that does not mean...
Oh how did it happen, I am so sorry for you
But I have to think of my self... of me
And she's the one I want

So will you please stay with me
I know I can make it worth your while
I can make it up to you
Life is give and take
Promises are meant to be broken
So will you, do you want to stay with me
I PROMISE I WON'T HURT YOU AGAIN
WILL YOU???
YES I WILL??

Ushanda io Elima

HOW CAN

how can i love
    a shallow man now
when i have known
    your depths

how can i want a cold man
    when i have felt your warmth
how can i want a hard man
    when i have cherished your softness
how can i want a soured man
    when i have tasted your sweetness
how can i want a callous man
    when i've received your kindness

how can i want a false man
    when i have trusted your tenderness
how can i want a blind man
    when i have entered your awareness
how can i want a dead man
    when i have touched your life

how can i accept
    a split and deadened you
when i have known
    you

Lorraine F. Joseph

I'M GOING

I told you one more lick
and this is it!
I'm going!

It's too late to apologize
Why should I believe your lies?
I'm going!

My bags are packed and sent.
And just now you can say I went!
I'm going!

Don't come no nearer.
I can't make it no ways clearer.
I'm going

What's love got to do with it?
You love me. I get hit.
I'm going!

Find somebody else to be beating on.
This one's gone.
You heard me right. I'm going, going, gone.

Dawn French

ROAD WORKS

I suppose
In a way
It was beautiful,
Black here
Rust there
Brown everywhere

I suppose
In a way
His soul was in the work
Cut here
Stick there
Rest every where

I never supposed
In any way
A road could look like
Grandma's quilt
Patch here
Patch there
Patch everywhere

Gladys Waterberg

POEM

Never before
the past
has been
such a
great future dream
than
when I met you
the first time
and wished
that the future
would never
become part
of the past

Carolle Grant

GARROTTE

If you paid an assassin to come after me
You couldn't have done better.
You and your thunderous stifling ways
Over the years seem laughable
Compared to pain I endured
For having discovered something sweet and unexplainable
Only to lose it as quickly.
Yes I feel pain, excruciating pain
And what pleasure it would give you
To mutter "Your sins are catching up with you kid".
What sins? What are sins?
Sins of a rich young Portuguese man dying at forty-two
An adventurous Scotsman drowning helplessly
Chatoyer falling under the sickly sword of Leith
Ancestors all catching up with me.
Sins — damn you all, how dare you condemn me
Me with no childhood
Always knowing, always feeling, wanting
Never really having
And now I die daily
Die because I discovered there could be something better
Only to have it withdrawn because I'm too damn complicated.
Did you hear that bugger?
Too damn complicated.
I bleed and your revenge is sweet
Fate has got me like no speeding bullet could
No blunt cutlass no dull-edged dagger
I am being strangled by feelings —
Feelings like I've never had with you.

Peggy Carr

MY OTHER LIFE

I wore our secret
 like a stolen garment
  and curled into its
   quiet moments when
   angry stares swirled
   cold around me

I trapped your touch
 inside
  and waited
   like a fugitive
    until the cruel hours
    tripped
     on the edge of dawn
     and tumbled into
      silence

then I'd unleash my
 memories of you
  and dare to smile
   as they lift me
   eagerly
    into another day
     where you wait with
     my other life
      stored safely in your
      eyes

MACHO MAN

You step out of
 your sleep each day
  and choose an image
  from the mirror
then you hurry
 to some new arena
  and gleefully incite
  desire

but your heart huddles
 with its fears
  in the shelter
   of your laughter
and no one cares
 to trace
  the hungry melody
   that sometimes strays
    into your rhapsody
     of casual kisses

DENIED

This love was meant
to pierce the sky
not stamped upon
and willed to die

Was meant to twine
about
the strong arch of
your mouth
and store its nectar
in your arms
not offered to the past
as alms

Still it climbs
starved alone it's true
but flowering
just for you

Washed holy in your
innocent eyes
it cannot die

And I

I will not cry

WHEN HE WENT AWAY

I packed his cases full of
cotton shirts
and thick warm nights
while he carefully
arranged his promises
in the windows of our future

Reverently I touched that morning
when he left
his farewell trailing
from a plane
and blending with
the chaste white fingers of
cooksmoke
which stole upward
through the dew to
wipe the smudges from the sky

How cheerfully our love moved out
to live inside
a cold blue envelope
and like an orphaned street-wise
child
slept easily
between two thin indifferent
lines

Like sheathed claws
atop a taut silk sheet
his first lies probed
the boundaries
of my innocence
then
artfully his words
rehearsed to
a finer edge
until
"winter"
"riots"
"strikes"
and
"Government"
flicked smoothly from his pen
to quiver
in my hopes

Carelessly he tried to patch
my still-hot pain
with random ten pound notes
and pictures
of some grey defiant
stranger

My letters drifted into
slow soliloquy
and reassured themselves
like Job

A velvet tongue of
tired midnight breeze
licked the moisture from
my cheeks
then shook an old newsheet
awake
snuggled underneath
and belched the flavour of
too many lonely women
on its breath

Today I forgot to
tremble
to the rhythm
of the postman's
bell

Hazel Simmons-McDonald

DRIFTWOOD

i skid off
driftwood pieces
on this empty shore
teetering on this tightrope
line of sea,
balanced
on this wave's crest
i am
fine-boned
some sudden
spurts of spray
calcified.

your mind turned
on a wave
in its green curve
i saw
grotesque
my shadow mirrored.
i had not thought
you could
so lucidly detail
this thing
so unfinely shaped
you say
is me.

waves turn
and i toss
a somersault in space
then slowly
as i drown i hear
your laugh
resounding
on and on...

Anielli J. Camrhal

INVITATION AU VOYAGE...

pour Anja

Venez
Fermez les yeux,
Laissez vous doucement
Guider
Sur ma barque
Corps en dérive
Venez
Donnez moi la main,
Laissez vous doucement
Emporter
Par les flots agités
De mes bras

Venez
Suivez moi,
Laissez vous doucement
Bercer
Par le roulis des
Milles plis de ma jupe

Venez
Venez
Laissez vous doucement
Envelopper
Dans l'arc en ciel
de mes yeux

Je vous emmènerai
A travers les flêches
Canne à sucre
Douce ivresse

Je vous conterai
Les récits de nos
Piquantes Matadores
De la Mangouste
Guerrière
Et de Reine Iguane
Alanguie au soleil

Je vous dirai
Le secret de nos coiffes
Les bruits de ma Terre
Coeur hospitalité

Je vous dévoilerai
La turquoise océane
L'émeraude tropicale
Pléntitude de l'être
Fermez les yeux
Donnez moi la main
Suivez moi
Doucement, Doucement
Venez
Venez...

INVITATION TO THE VOYAGE ...

for Anja

Come
Close your eyes
Gently let go
Follow my guide on this boat
a body drifting

Come
Give me your hand
Gently let go
Be carried away
By the rough seas
of my arms

Come
Follow me
Gently let go
Be cradled
By the rolling
of the many folds of my skirt

Come
Come
Gently let go
Be surrounded
By the rainbow
of my eyes

I will take you
Over the masts
Sugar cane
Sweet drunkenness

I will tell to you
The stories of our
Racy matadors
Of the mongoose
Amazon-warrior
And the Iguana Queen
Basking in the sun

I will reveal
the secrets of our headdresses
the rumours of my Earth
her welcoming heart

I will unveil
an ocean of turquoise
the tropic's emerald
A fullness of being

Close your eyes
Give me your hand
Follow me
Gently, gently
Come
Come ...

[1] *From the title of the 19th century French poet Baudelaire's
"Invitation au Voyage" which romanticized merchant ships in
harbour as great possibilities for escape.*

Elaine Savory

TO ALL OTHER WOMEN WHO HOBBLE THEMSELVES

for w.

how comforting
and bleak
always to want the men
who fail me
or who are distant
spiked by ambition
or otherwise excused
from passionate conviction

of course
i could say
i am married
to my work
if it convinced you

somewhere
i just fear
there is a man
who might say
something definite
set up my typewriter
so that i fall on it
at waking
cuddle me up
in unmistakable appreciation
have no mothers in closets
no blunt and rusting sabres
in suitcases
under the bed
no voice which becomes
gentle on telephones
loving after four rums

would i then
have accounts
at all the airlines
and a plan?

Christine Craig

CODA

Poor woman, the man's truth
is an empty yabba for you.
Vainly you try to fill it
with a swirling, shifting
liquid of your own.

Where can we meet my brother,
my lover, my friend
to make something new together.

> I will meet you on the road
> for I have done with waiting.
> I will help you with your load
> and welcome your greeting.
> I will meet you on the road
> for I have shaped my journey.

The Exile

Madeline Coopsammy

IN THE DUNGEON OF MY SKIN

In Suez they thought I was Egyptian
In Manitoba they wonder if I'm native-born
In India they say derisively:
Indian Christian! Goan! Anglo-Indian!
In the Bronx, wayside vendors spoke to me
In the guttural music of Cervantes and Borges
A long time ago, in my native place
on coral shores beside the Pirate's Main
they said, "You surely must be Spanish."
In a country famous for its indiscriminate racial copulation
ethnic nomenclature was the order of the day
and "Spanish"
was a mantle that gathered in its folds
all who bore or seemed to bear some trace,
however faint, of European ancestry.
It labelled you a cut above
the blacks and Hindus, low men on the totem pole;
rendered you a more pleasing place in the racial mosaic.

Now though the landscape of my being
negates the burnished faces of my youth
while molten rhythms
forged from the heart of Africa and India
elude me now
and I have cast from consciousness
satiric folk-songs spawned from the tortured metres of our
bastard English tongue
have clipped the bonds of cultures and boundaries
and made myself a universal woman
yet this poor frame, no castle
proves itself no fortress, but a dungeon from which
there can be no release.

THE SECOND MIGRATION

Was it the bloody-minded Kali
or the many-handed Shiva
who thought it fit to lead us
from the green wastes of the Indo-Gangetic
to the sweet swards of the Caroni
then in a new migration
to Manitoba's alien corn?
they never thought to state
the price to be exacted
or how or where it would be paid.
Images of a just society dangled
tantalizingly before our eyes
we thought that here at last and now at last
the spectres of colour
would never haunt
our work, our children's lives our play
that in the many-faceted mosaic
we, angled and trimmed to fit
would find ourselves our corner of the earth.
How could we not know
that time, which heals
just as frequently destroys
and like the sixties flower darlings
we, too, would soon become anachronisms
reminders of a time
a time of joy and greening
we are the mistakes of a liberal time
you did not really court us, it is true
rather, purging us with neon-coloured pills of
medicals and points and two official languages
your tolerant humanity
festered woundings of "brain drain"
while our leaders pleaded, impotent in agony
"Do not take our best!"
"We want your best,
No Notting Hills for us," you warned.
And so again we crossed an ocean
convinced that little Notting Hills we'd never be.

Now lounging in our bite-sized backyards
and pretending that we do not see
the curling vapours of our neighbour's burger feast
(the third this week)
borne on the Prairie wind
across the picket fence
we ask ourselves now far we are
from San Juan, Belmont and St. James.

Meiling Jin

STRANGERS IN A HOSTILE LANDSCAPE

When people ask me where I come from
I tell them this story.

I was born in the Southern Hemisphere
in the early hours of the morning
when night exchanges with day
and the light gains ascendancy.
What I have to say is brief,
so listen,
and make of it what you will.

When my grandmother was a girl,
paddle-boats crossed the river
from the town.
They brought all sorts of people
looking for
God only knows what.
Unspeakable riches, I suppose.
Instead, they found sugar-cane;
sugar-cane and mosquitoes.
They worked hard on large plots of land
dem call plantation.
Slaves worked the plantations originally
and when slavery was abolished,
freed slaves worked the plantations.
And when they were decimated,
we worked the plantations.
We were called,
indentured labourers

My grand-father sailed on the ship
Red-riding Hood:
part of a straggly band
of yellow humanity.
They severed the string
that tied them to the dragon,
and we grew up never knowing
we belonged
to a quarter of the world's people.

A damn plot you might think.
Yes indeed, it was called,
colonial-ization,
spelt with a z.
The prince of the plot was called Brit Ain
but actually, he had many brothers,
Holl And, France and so on.
They fought each other occasionally,
but essentially, they were intent
on making themselves rich
thro' robbery and by brain-washing us.
They stole from us.
And at the same time,
sung psalms,
Such sweet psalms
and sung so well
wash the sweat and tears away.

After much time
and many millions of £s later,
they leased us back our land
through a deed called In-Dee-pendence.
This meant the land was ours,
but everything we produced,
was theirs.
We even got our own leaders:
men of great worth
to them.

Meanwhile,
another plot called Imperial-Ization
had worked its way through the world
and the earth was carved up
and re-aligned.

Back on the Plantation,
we all fought each other
(with a little help from out side).
We squabbled over what would remain
when the In-Dee-pendence deed was passed
and the prince departed for home.

And so,
in the midst of the troubles,
my parents packed their bags.
They followed the general recruitment drive
to the imperial palace itself.

We arrived in the Northern Hemisphere
when Summer was set in its way
running from the flames that lit the sky
over the Plantation.
We were a straggly bunch of immigrants
in a lily white landscape.
We made our home among strangers,
knowing no one but ourselves.

When I was a girl
I lived in a box
that is why, my head is square.
I lived on jam
and played on the streets
I survived in this hostile landscape.

And when one day
I was chased from school
I turned and punched their teeth out.
Too harsh, you say,
I don't agree,
they would have smashed
my head in.
One day I learnt
a secret art,
Invisible-Ness, it was called.
I think it worked
as even now, you look
but never see me.

I was born in the Southern Hemisphere
in the early hours of the dawn
and when I die
I shall return
to a place I call my own.
Only my eyes will remain
to watch and to haunt,
and to turn your dreams
to chaos.

THE KNOCK

Where shall I lay my head?
House and home have I none,
Nor country yet to call my own.
Once I thought my home was here,
But now I'm told that
By some Act,
I have no right to live
in peace.

I have been
right round the globe.
Not a traveller by choice,
But one who has been dispossessed.

I live in fear of the knock
That knows no mercy.
Swift and suddenly it comes,
And I, behind the door,
Wait trembling.

And quietly comes the Dawn.
The knock.
Police.
A short trip
Via the airport.
A oneway ticket
To an unknown place
Called Homelands.

Grace Nichols

WE NEW WORLD BLACKS

The timbre
in our voices
betrays us
however far
we've been

whatever tongue
we speak
the old ghost
asserts itself
in dusky echoes
like driftwood
traces

and in spite of
ourselves
we know the way
back to

the river stone

the little decayed
spirit
of the navel string
hiding in our back garden

Aimée Eloidin

HANTISE

L'exil ne pardonne pas
L'exil est sans pitié!
Marquée à tout jamais
Traumatisée à perpétuité!
Parfois je rêve de grands espaces
Parfois je revois Sainte-Genes
Parfois j'ai envie de crier
Je pense: ce n'était pas si mal!
Poutant quand j'y étais
Il m'arrivait souvent de pleurer
Il m'arrivait souvent de rêver
J'étais mélancolique et angoissée
Alors, il m'arrivait d'implorer Dieu:
Fais surtout que je ne crève pas ici
Mon âme y serait bien trop triste!
Et alors je pensais aux miens
Et surtout je penais à Elle!
Et plus j'y pensais, plus j'en souffrais!
Plus j'y pensais, plus j'en mourrais!
J'avais mal de ma Martinque
Je la désirais
J'en crevais!

Quatre ans se sont écoulés
Depuis que je l'ai retrouvée
Mais ces rêves continuent
à hanter mes nuits!
Talence, Saint-Genès, Mérignac...

HAUNTED

Exile gives no pardon
Exile has no pity!
Forever branded
Neverending shock!
At times I dream of open spaces
At times I see Saint-Genes
At times I feel like weeping
I think: it wasn't so bad!
And yet, when I was there
I would often cry
I would often daydream
Melancholy and anguish were mine
And then, I implored God:
O please don't let me die here
My soul would surely be too sad
And I would think of my loved ones
And especially of Her
And the more I thought, the more I suffered
And the more I thought, the more I thought I would die
I was sick of my Martinique
I wanted her
She was killing me

Four years run past
Since I've found her again
But these dreams still
haunt my nights
Talence, Saint-Genes, Merignac

Margaret D. Gill

BRIDGE

Restore me, Adéwoulé.
Bring me to potions mixed
with whispers I barely remember.
Bring me to rivers whose names
I stumble in recalling
Recall me rituals whose magic
lies buried in 300 years
of prudent forgetting
and forced burials,
and coerced mythologies.
'You do not know'
'You do not know' what separation is
You who conquer the oceans in jet planes
and purchase your own tickets.
'A hard coming we had of it.'
Now restore me to rivers and mountains
and kingdoms and history.
Restore me 'old humanities'.
Fortify ancestral memories to shore me
against this future.

Note: *Adéwoulé is an African name meaning "the crown has come
back to this house".*

Zoila M. Ellis

SNATCHES

Black Sambo!
Black Sambo!
How di lee bwoy head so hard
fi comb? Tough head
jus' like i wutless daddy
wid 'i bad-up nigga-ways.
Yu year say Benji married?
'im ketch way lee spanish gyal.
Yes dahling Benji di look fi upgrade
'im colour...

Black Sambo!
Black Sambo!

Snatches of memory
a little child prays:
God, bless ma an
sen Pa home an
bless baby and bredda an John an
mek me
like snow —
white
like Dick an Jane.......

Snatches of Memory
the smell of burning rubber
the sound of car doors slamming
the sight of the street
littered with the rags and
guts of a nobody
and someone shouting
"don't trouble the tourist, man
he didn't see!"
Nobody saw.........

So we leave the sight
the sound of these
to the music makers
the flag wavers
keep the Dread despair below........

Nomads in a desert
of our being
the way behind each footprint
is the last
there is no past
there is hope........

Ushanda io Elima

FROM EXILE

I don't live
  in the city.
Cities and towns
  are just prisons
Where I await
  my release,
Where I wait
  'till I'm free again
To live —
  in the bush
  in my forests
  my wilderness.
Dear Creator,
  Nature-Mother,
I sing gratefulness
  and praise!
So wild and sweet
  you welcome me
Back in your heart,
  always.
Someday I'll stay.

Judith Behrendt

"MANIWAUMA": For Simon

Two sweet brown boys
Walking on their way to school
In short khaki pants
Thin, scarred legs extended
To flies, to scrapes, to pain
Vulnerable.

They walk dutifully
(As if marching)
Past coconut palms
Past the blue angry sea
To a school where they are taught
The language of submission,
of humiliation, fear, futility.

Inside they march to a different tune
The one that runs through their minds
Is persistent, rhythmic,
like the drum at a nine night.
A noble people, dignified,
It beats in their very bood
Almost frightening in its intensity.

They often burst into tears,
Not knowing why.
Then they hold, caress,
Console each other,
Telling each other "Maniwauma",
And patting each other
Like a mother "scolding" a babe
That's cried for too long
(The child forgetting why it started)
"Little men" (growing into manhood together)

Wiping away tears
Crying because of an unfillable loneliness,
And from the cruel denial
Of allowing them to be
Who they are.

The sky darkens as they walk
Deep grey clouds lowering on the horizon
It will rain soon.
They must hurry or teacher will lash them
Huge raindrops fall from the sky
And mingle with their own small tears.

Note: Maniwauma means "Be quiet" in the Garifuna Black Carib language.

Randi Gray Kristensen

BEFORE THE END

The walls are closing in
here in city centre
centre city
of a foreign land.

The plants, at least
have sense enough to turn
towards the window
whenever a huge, unyielding hand
has turned them away.

I stand beside them
this lonely Sunday
and stare at the alley
furnished in gray
identical windows,
home smells
float from the kitchen
home calls
deep in the heart
as we
foreign palm and unwilling tree
stand by a window
gazing on gray.

WHAT WE DO WHEN WE MEET

Of course, we talk of home
building sandcastles on an exile shore
one eye
on the banana leaf
brown with blight
planted in the shade of an elm tree
on someone else's main street.

In desperate hope
we share a breadfruit
out of a tin
bought from the corner store
But it never tastes the same
as the ripe
green
fruit
toasted over cane trash
on an iron grill by the kitchen door
and the words we share
are twisted
as though forced
through the cassava press
to extract every ounce of poison
to leave only the whole
the edible
the nutritious heart of the matter.

The bars remain a fence between us
A drop or two of poison
slips through
dilute enough
to leave unaffected
all but those who would know
(us)

And so we speak of home
a canvas of watercolours
and ardent speeches
smeared
by a drop or two of the sap
dripping
in the shade of an elm tree
on someone else's main street.

SOMEWHERE IS SUMMER

Somewhere is summer
This we know with a precision
the ancients never dreamed of
nor needed to.

The old one, shivering,
wrapped in rags,
crone bent over
a beechwood cane,
stands in the dying light
wind-whipped
as she gazes at the field,
dry
and empty,
and mutters —
"goddess forgive
your daughter's betrayal.
Our hearts wither with you
and pray her safe return.
Youth and beauty
the blinding curse
only one who lives in darkness
could hope to hold.
Even his hold must loose
she will return
summer is somewhere" —
mutters the crone
and slowly stoops
to gather acorns
and pine-cones
for the mid-winter dance.

Jane King Hippolyte

INTERCITY DUB

for Jean

Brixton groans —
From the horror of the hard weight
Of history
Where the whites flagellate
In their ancestry
And the blacks hold the stone
And they press it to their hearts
And London is a hell
In many many parts.
But your voice rings true
From the edge of hell
Cause the music is the love
And you sing it so well.

And I travel through the country
On the inter-city train
And the weather may be bad
But the sperm of the rain
Wriggles hope, scribbles hope
Cross the windows of the train
And the autumn countryside
Has a green life still
And the rain-sperm says
It will come again, it will
It will come again
New rich life from the bitter
And dark and driving rain —
And you run like water
Bringing light through the walls
Like the water you connect
With the light above
Like the water writing making
The green life swell
Cause the music is the love
And you sing it so well.

Now I cannot give to you
What you gave to me
But one small part
Of your bravery
Makes me stand up to say
That I want to make them see
That you showed me the way
That the way is you
And the way is we.
And the love is in the water
In the wells pooled below
And the love is in the light
And the rain lances down
From the light to the well
And it points to heaven
And it points to hell
And the love is real
Make the music swell
Cause the music is the love
And you sing it so well.

There's a factory blowing smoke-rings
Cross the railway line
You know it took me time to learn
That this country wasn't mine
And I want to go back home
To swim in the sunset bay
Feel the water and the light
Soft-linking night and day
Like the music makes a bridge —
But there's joy here too
And I might not have seen it
If I hadn't heard you.
And I hope now I'll be writing
This poem all my life
For the black city world
Where the word is a knife
That cuts through the love
And divides up the life.
For you saved me from a trap
Just before I fell
Cause music is the love
And you sing it so well.

The Brixton-battered sisters
Hissed their bitterness and hate
With their black man the oppressor
And death the white race fate
And they don't want to build
No bridge no gate —
And I nearly turned back
Till I heard your voice
Ringing clarion-clear
And you burst like a flower
From the sad sad soil
And you blew like a breeze
Round the shut-tight hall
And you danced like a leaf
And you sang like a bell —
You said Music reaches heaven
And music changes hell
Cause the music is the love
And you sing it so well.

Audrey Ingram-Roberts

POEM II

for Duckie Simpson of "Black Uhuru"

Well charged, halfway between generations
of impotent anger and languid nonchalance,
you smile at the irony that "I' n I are lazy"
for it took all your yesterdays of industry
to middle the passage between Rema and Jungle.

So long Rastafari call you, yet here you recline
with affected ease, locksed in the barrel of
Babylonian markets, captive to strategy.
So long you'd been away from home and the problems
of travel from Waterhouse to Constant Spring.
Now, bucking the pass, too grassed to fear the
youths of Englington spawned in violence,
or the duppy gunmen, uniformed for crime.

Well charged, you bus' it pon Red, free,
spaced out in raw control, Uhuru dread in
Babylon, Ja, Paris, London!
Sponged in reggae, seeped deep in pungent herbs
I glide above the undulating hills to see you
reach beyond with deft assurance and grasp a
life outside the violence that spawned you.

Well charged, I watch you grow, trusting that
you too, like Cliff, Marley, Toots, will show
another way to the coke ruptured youths obedient
to the orders of the remington.
Hard of hearing above the cacophony of nothing
to lose or gain, in the violence that spawned them.

Michelle Cliff

LOVE IN THE THIRD WORLD

exists
Love in the Third World can be just as powerful/complicated/
multileveled/varied/long-standing
as in the First or Second Worlds — maybe more so.
as on the moons of Jupiter
or through the dusty rings of Saturn — maybe more so.
in the blood-red canals of Mars
the clouded circumference of Venus
the tumultuous speck of hot Mercury — maybe more so.
as much as on the dangerous surface of Uranus
through the wild orbit of Neptune
or on distant dependable Pluto — maybe more so.

A Jamaican woman visits home and returns with a photograph.
Two women live together in a structure made of packing crates
behind the Kingston Parish Church. She met one of them on a
bus and was invited to dinner. The women arrange the contents
of their crates for company and build a fire where they make
yam and banana and salted codfish. Their King James sits on an
upended Ovaltine box — a prize from someone's Sunday
School. The women cover another box with a piece of crocus

sack and serve their meal on flattened milk tins and cracked enamel utensils cleaned under the city standpipe nearby. At least, the photographer says, they have each other.

Yes. But the simple and final and flat question is why — on this Black island-nation, our motto being "out of many, one people" — are two Black women living as they must. And it does not really matter whether their crates are labeled Westinghouse or General Electic or Purveyors to Her Majesty the Queen. Please don't tell me it's very complicated or that there will always be people like these who choose to live on city streets. Don't tell me that if it hadn't been for the shanties Bob Marley would never have existed. Don't tell me the climate causes such distress, but if we are warm we can't be truly miserable. Or that the trees bear for everyone and there are windfalls to be gathered if only our people weren't so lazy.

I know the price of cooking oil and rice.
I know the price of Blue Mountain coffee and Canadian saltfish.
I have a sense of the depth of our self-hatred.
I speak from a remove of time and space — I have tried to hold your shape and history within me. I keep track of you through advertisements and photographs. Through *The Harder They Come* and "Natty Dread." By entering the patty shops in Bedford-Stuyvesant. By watching a group of applepickers stroll through a Massachusetts hilltown. Through the shots of graffitti on the walls of Tivoli Gardens. My homeland. My people.

I wonder if I will ever return — I light a cigarette to trap the fear of what returning would mean. And this is something I will admit only to you. I am afraid my place is at your side. I am afraid my place is in the hills. This is a killing ambivalence. I bear in mind that you with all your cruelties are the source of me, and like even the most angry mother draw me back.

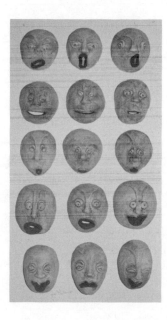

The Mourner

Ahdri Zhina Mandiela

MIH FEEL IT

(Wailin fih Mikey)

Dih dred ded
an it dun suh?
No sah

dih dred ded
an it dun suh?

> Ow can a man
> kill annadah one
> wid stone
> cold-
> bludded intenshan
>
> rockstone
> bludgeon im ead
> an
> im drop dung ded
> an nuh one
> nuh awsk
> why
> such a wikkid
> wikkid tawsk
> should
> anna-
> nyah-
> late
> dih dred

Dih dred ded
an it dun suh?
no sah

dih dred ded
an it dun suh?

Early early
inna dih day
Mikey ah trod
dung a illy way

isite up sum men
from a pawty fence
an hence-
forth
was stopped!
wid all dih
chattin whe gwaan
an questions ensued
Mikey painin run out
ah im mout
too soon!
an is den dih trouble
run out

for BAM!
four stone inna dem ans
an BAM!
dem lik Mikey dung
an
mih feel it
mih feel it
mih feel it

Dih dred ded an it dun suh?
no sah
dih dred ded
an it dun suh?

ones must know
dih reasons
for dis deadly
assault
committed
out of season
no reason
dred dred dred dred
season

'Riddemshan for every dred
mus cum
riddemshan
mus cum'

is dih livity
not dih rigidity
for even doah seh
Mikey ded
cause dem mash up
im ead
even doah seh
Mikey gawn
im spirit trod awn
trod awn
tru: RIDDEMSHAN

'Riddemshan for every dred
mus cum
riddemshan
mus cum'
Dih dred ded
as it dun suh? ´
NO SAH!

Vanda Radzik

LINGUISTICS #3

JUNE 13th: BLACK SUNFLOWERS

a star turns inward
when it dies
and a whole new quest is born;

each dark time, my love
is a direction to understanding
the particular terror of that time

this world is a garden of contradiction
black sunflowers grow at the heart of it;
the sun's eclipse is a rite of passage

time will yet come
yes, when
flowers will not bend their heads in awful sorrow
black sunflowers full blown
heightened in dreadful beauty
outbid all glare of steel
and in their perfect darkness
confront the certain light
this day, each year, every time.

Lynette Atwell:

THE DYING OF AN OLD FRIEND

I looked at her,
And saw death written on her face,
Her eyes bulged,
And the pain wrenched
Her face into endless grimaces,
And I continued to gaze,
Into the face of courage,
When all I wanted was to run from there,
The fragile body,
Belly extended,
With that murderous growth,
Yet she could talk to me,
Me for whom there was no solace,
And for the first time,
I face the unrelenting steady force of death,
Not crises,
But a slow wearing down of body,
Of twisted face,
And darkened hand,
Of spiky legs,
Too weak to hold her up,
But yet her eyes kept riveting me to the chair,
And I stayed,
And we spoke,
Of trivia,

And all the while,
Death sat mocking me,
But she,
So brave and serene,
Was comforting me,
With her strength and faith,
And she made me wonder,
At all the small things that used to rend my heart,
She who was retreating,
With such dignity.

Velma Pollard

TWO FOR NEVILLE

I.

The fisherman closes his net
the sailor is home from the sea
goodnight Jim
goodnight Jack
goodnight Josefina

If you go home
don't ask for me
or anyone
Just wait and read each morning's
In Memoriam
where every column
prints
some keen fresh face
you only think of on a bicycle
grinning like mad
in one dimension

Old age
is not the sitting and recounting tales
is not the leisure to enjoy your friends
They lied who spoke of endless sunsets
And they knew better
they had lived the wars
and those familiar suitcases
sent back as
luggage unaccompanied

Learn how the moving finger writes...
these lessons come too quick and sharp
to our unreadiness
life is a river only because
so many little streams
touch end to end
What gives it meaning?
that's the philosopher's trip
and whether he gazes on a stone
or a lightbulb
or a peeny-wally
There's nothing he will know
unless the Great Mind
takes him in His trust
shows him the masterplan
so large
so comprehensive
he won't understand
and so he still won't know

No one philosophy can answer all
each man is an island
each mind is a muffin tin
and so we sit with our invisible pencils
working out strategies
to cope with brevity
to cope with our adieux
to love — too sweet to forget
to life — too intensive to leave
but most
to friends and friendships
mangroves of our shelter
stuck with benches everywhere
saying
'now tell me...'

II.

The man was ready
he had his Jerusalem Bible
marked off at a page
warning us to be ready
every yesterday

And because he was an artist
it's the psalmist's word he took
'My days (are) listed and determined
even before the first of them occurred'

Awareness is all
Something had touched him
some event
had put him on a thought path
few suspect.
Unlikely...

Every Sunday
shirtsleeves and tie
the weekday jeansman
reading the lesson
passing the velvet bag
and 'peace be unto you
and you
and you'

Peace be unto you
my friend and brother
for I-ver

Hazel Simmons-McDonald

TRAGIC MUSE

How these letters fascinate!
I marvel at them, and marvel more

That she, in the hey-day of her morning
Let down her veils and smiled,
Shrugged the universe off her side.
For this she'd stayed the dawn

And made a poem of her morning.
Mark how the frenzied images drift!

Shrouded in veils
The lady sits pondering the act.

In the city somewhere,
While he carps and doubts

My lady agitates her heart.
Unheeding infant cries, she rises slowly, turns on the gas.

Lately, he gathered her images
Marbled her thoughts on bleached leaves of yew.

Little comfort that he thinks
His pill more bitter than fumes

That brought sweet heaven
Crashing about her ears.

PARTING

Death came quickly
as a foetus
suddenly spewed
from its mother's womb
while brief sun blazed
at its zenith
burning placenta
in the fecund earth.

He stood
against his shadow's feet
and looked
at wind-waved
funeral sheets
over your frozen feet.
Death had come
too soon
introduced in
a single tear
and left
as soon
his shadow long behind him
stretching after-birth pains
in the wake of
the dying sun
taking another son
in his descent.

Christine Craig

ST. ANN SATURDAY

Saturday afternoon. So many shades
of black swinging down the road.
funeral time.
Nice afternoon she get eh!

If.

An so many smady turn out
like a ole days funeral

Dats right.

Imagine her time come
so quick. Well, de Lord giveth
an de Lord taketh away.

Sure ting.

Children walk lightly, plaits
floating with rainbows of ribbons
beside auntie's strong hips, uncle's
suit so dark his body is held in tight,
moves only back, front, front, back.
Auntie's hips roll sedately, heave
like waves beside the dancing plaits.

You see her big daughter come from
Canada. Me no like how she look
at all. No sir. She look a way.
Me never member say she so mawga.
Me mind tell me she catching
hard times over dere.

Maybe so an maybe not.

Imagine is six pickney Miss Martha
raise, she one bring dem up an
send dem into de world.
Six pickney, she one.
Well as I say she send dem
out an is one degge, degge
daughta come home fe bury her.
Still an all, dem neva come
when she was hearty, no mek sense
dem come when she direckly dead.

A dat too.

Starapple leaves, double toned
bend quiet over the steady walking,
walking for Miss Martha, gone to rest.
The path she walked, food to market,
children to school, Sunday to church,
steady walking. In the end, alone
under the starapple leaves a hush
fell over her, silence of age
of no names left to call
to table. Of no news from
Delroy or Maisie or Petal
or Lennie or Edith or Steve.

Nice turn out Miss Martha have.
See Mass Len clear from Topside.
An no Granny Bailey dat from Retreat?
Well I neva. Tink seh she dead
long time. Time passing chile
we all moving down de line weself.

True word.

Karin Ammon

DEATH

A sudden flare of light opened my mind
as the thread of life was slipping away
from my moisture-covered palms.
Before me rose the picture of my fifth birthday party.
There I was, standing on a stool,
my eyes over-bright, mischievous yet innocent,
my cheeks rosy from the candles' glow.
My mother's voice saying,
"Come now dear, blow out the candles and make a wish."
Yet as I puffed up my cheeks with air,
pursed my lips and blew,
I killed myself,
and Death hung like the wisps of smoke
spiralling from the five tiny birthday candles.

FROM A HOSPITAL BED

Fear, nausea, darkness...
The white blinds my blinking eyes
The smell of antiseptic invades my nostrils
The questions hammer on my brain.
The scream strangles my throat
Let me out! Let me out!
But it is killed with the prick of a needle
which dulls my senses and strangely calms my writhing limbs.

Yet, as the hours tick by,
and the months are pulled off the calendar
Hope is no longer my companion
Pain with his selfish arms, binds my body with iron bands.
Break, I scream voicelessly
Let me out! Let me out!
The white coats surround me
all armed with sharp instruments.
The battle has begun,
The sweat is flowing
The pain is increasing
Let me out! Let me out!
But a sudden flare of light
A shape, a face, a beckoning finger
The love is showing
The smile is welcoming
Let me in Lord, let me in.

Gladys August Hall

DEATH AND THE LIVING

In memory of Mother

She lay there
Breathing heavily
Eyes closed and no
            awareness of what was going on.
I wiped her brow
                and gave her smelling salts
And wondered what good these were doing.
I felt her feet,
        her body,
                her arms
I knew death was fast approaching —
For these were very cold.
Her neck
        and head
            were hot —
                    very hot.

When those got cold, I concluded,
Death would take its toll.
But the oxygen helped keep my hopes high.
Doctor said he'd try.

A few hours passed,
The breathing was less rapid,
The sweat so profuse
         The whole human form
               shaped on the bedclothes —
And all the while I stood there.
I couldn't believe
         I was watching her die.
I touched her again and again.
So cold,
         so very cold.
Is death so cold?

I left her.
Few minutes passed
         then I returned.

"Nurse: Please see this patient."
The thought raced through my mind
         before the nurse could come —
'Death is silent,
         Death is quick.
         Death is ashamed to have the living see her die'.

"She's dead:
         But the doctor must certify."
I closed her eyes
And watched the peace
         upon her face.
I did not cry.
I could not.
Yet it was hard to comprehend
How death lives among the living.

I thought of God's goodness.
Every day He gives —
But the day He takes away
The questions mount up high.
But surer than many things —
                              sometime,

                                        somehow,

It brings to everyone
                The realization
That death lives among the living.

Margaret Watts

TO SABINA AT HER FUNERAL

I.

After the mourning service
choristers come
to your home.
The women's group
sings —
your family
in black
your children
in wonder.
Your sister
intones
a dirge.
Your husband
in dignity
reaps condolences
biding
his terrible time.
A black suited uncle
in tie
faints
in the heat
and strange garb.

Young girls
shield tears
and lust
under floppy black hats.
The clan head
guards
the tasteless
cedi salad
tossed on the table.
At the crowd's fringe
your restless sons
pace
back and forth.
Your childless friend
stares
at your nine
and drinks
to stave off
the grief
and lechery.

II.

I,
a stranger
to you
and your world
resist
the ritual demands
of your death,
chafe
in the mid-day sun
and the sorrow
half-wondering
full-knowing
why I have come.
Sister,
I mourn you
in awe
unafraid
of your ghost.

In my dirge
I call you
faithful
Methodist
commonsense
hymn-singing
true loving mother,
teach me again
to feed my child,
exhort me again
to dress discreetly,
tie up my hair,
behave like a mother,
I call you.
Come back.
Live in your children.

Show the liberated
what we have lost.

Ruth Sawh

DEATH

This time you were expected at this house
    Oh death
No surprises, no shocks, no ambushes
    as you sometimes stage
Just a gradual, menacing, cruel grip
You dawdled with time and cursed it
    with your stenchful breath
And now you come, retarded sinner
    of sinners.

Martha Tjoe-Nij

LAST WISHES

(to Mathilda 15 MRT 1986)

last wishes sound
like hissing snakes
sliding into the grave

aimlessly thunderous waves
echo life and love
across the shoreline

through morning mist
death's rattling anchor
sinks deeper into the flesh

At sunset
lifeless last wishes
stir the funeral flag.

Zoila M. Ellis

REQUIEM OF SORROW

Hush, Beloved, hush,
Let the wind
whisper a birdsong
to the turbulent falls
Breaking and tumbling frenzy
on bonewhite boulders
Bringing its pain to rest
in silent pools
Can you add more?

See it gather to itself
Casuarinas
Shrieking
crescendos of grief —
to the starless skies
until
the torrents drain the world of tears...
Red Hibiscus bleed
softly over grave mounds
mourning until evening,
Always remembering...

Rutheen Taylor

DEATH IS A CROOKED STILE

What is this "stairway to heaven"
death borne souls may climb?
Is heaven some celestial attic
where Earth's discarded lives are kept?
Is it packed with musty memories?
Are cobwebs spun in its rafters?
And does dust settle in rusty locks
that are closed for eternity?

No —

Death is a crooked stile
leading down to Earth again.
And heaven is a dream
in the hearts of living man.

If we would know what heaven is
we must build it here.
We must gather our materials
and spread them in the sun.
They are the things we love most —
fields of awakening seeds,
the peace of a child's slumber
after his needs are satisfied,
the pulse of young, ripe blood
feeling joy in accomplishment,
a kiss, a smile or a song
where discords are resolved
into harmonies,
experience rich in years,
and the conviction
that life is sacred.

For —

Death is a crooked stile
leading down to Earth again.
And heaven is a dream
in the hearts of living man.

The Land

Ruffina Lee Sheng Tin

LET ME

Let me hide my hair in your sands
Cover myself in your white ribboned lace
Let my touch linger with your wingèd playmates
My pale skin colour with your bronze-washed tans

Let me muse at clouds sailing past
And watch from beneath, the sky-blue vast
My feet to feel the kiss of your tides
My face to tingle on your salty sides

Let me float in your moss-green buoyancy
Tossed on your waves of rippled beauty
Drown my ear with the cry of your gull
Swooping down swiftly at the unaware cod

Let me stand on your water-sculptured cliffs
And gaze on your mermaids and water nymphs
Then I too will whistle with your coastal winds...
One song richer my heart would have been

Deborah Singh-Ramlochan

POUI

Through my back door
wide vistas open before me
rolling hummocky
green carpeted hills

A yellow poui
young
yet blazing in colour
scattered teardrops of sunshine
How I yearned to have
just one branch
I asked you
but you said the tree
was in another person's land

Evening
I come home
and rush to the back door
heavy rains fell today
now there are no more
poui blossoms
all battered
lost to earth

Leonie Kessell

JELLY-FISH

A dinner plate of jello pulsing through the sea
Why, it's nothing but a jelly-fish!
Look again
The transluscent, colourless dome is patterned
With a four leaf clover
A corded outline in fuchsia pink
And around the dome is a skirt
A silken fringe, so fine spun
It appears as the water itself
Extruded into light rays.
Beneath the dome hangs a mass
Of breathing tissue, an aurora of gathered ribbon.
This wondrous colony of changeling parts
Undulates towards the surface of the sea
Until its back touches the light
A shiver of shock in the strange air element
And it rolls away and down again
Into the cool green depths.
The commune of the jelly fish
Knows no argument, no strife, no
"I want to be boss today"
A placid, ordered group of the well behaved.
But does the jelly fish know about pleasure?
Does it pulse in ecstasy and delight?
Does it twist in fear down there in the deep?
Neutrons piercing its cells bringing about
Old age and death?
Or is the jelly fish a world in
A galaxy, in a universe eternally expanding?
Its world calling to other worlds?
Emitting strange signals, unheard and unheeded.
Look again — why, it's nothing but a jelly fish!

Evelyn St. Hill

EARLY MORNING

At the crack of dawn
There is the sound of water running
in buckets
Also the chirp chirping of birds
outside in the morning air
The mewing of a kitten
The crying of babies nearby
The whistling of kettles
The smell of kerosene oil
The smell of frying plantains
in coconut oil.
The neighing of horses
being groomed for their morning duties
The beating and washing of clothes
under yard pipes
The blare of radios
giving out the latest news or
the latest Indian tunes.

Ruth Sawh

MORNING

I'd rather eat a cucumber during the
    morning of its life
Before its refreshing crispness
Grows limp and stale with age

And so, I'd rather use a dewy
    fresh morning
While pearls of dew between blades
    of grass still cradle
When I can savour the birth of breezes and
Before that delicious cucumber morning
Is sliced too thinly for me to have a
    healthy share.

Cheza Dailey

MOTHER NATURE IS ANGRY!

Mother Nature
   Is
   Angry!
I heard her roaring
   by the sea side

Why are you so upset?
   is it my brother
   the one who understands
   all about destruction
   and does not live
   according to the law

I tried to tell her
   It's not me
      doing these things

I pray to my father
      please protect me
            from my Mother's wrath
      I only want to kiss her
            and feel her gentleness
                  once again
                        caressing my structure

But she would not let me hear
      not even to touch her skirt
      she'd whirl it up, and lash me, not hurting me
            just enough to keep me in my place

Mother Nature
   Is
   Angry

She was waving
      her hands all up in the air
            swelling up, beating the shore
                  like a drummer
                        But I could not dance with her
                              the way I wanted

She told me to step aside
    While she scolded all her naughty disrespectful children
    And if I were to come into the punishment room
        during their spankings — I would get licks too

        She will drown them
            with her tears
        And burn them with spit
    For they have defiled her very womb
            And bitten off her breasts

Mother Nature
    Is
    Angry!!!

Phyllis Punnett

DROUGHT

The leafless trees stand stark against the sky
like sentinels of doom, and all around
the blackbirds wheel, and caw and cry,
their mournful dirges drifting to the ground,
so parched and dry beneath the burning sun,
it's brazen glare reflected on the brown
and brittle grass when morning comes.

And all day long the people hurry by
with pails in hand, in frenzied quest of water
seeping through the sand, or even in a
dried-up river bed. Beneath a stone there
lies a little pool, spreading its wetness
across the dusty earth, to where a lone
lizard sits, drowsing in the cool.

Comes the night, and casts her mantle over all
our tears, that this, our green and beauteous land
should turn into a desert, the hillsides seared
by flames that sweep across when darkness falls.
The bush fires glow like lamps in the evening air,
the gray smoke billowing, and rising up
to heaven with our prayers.

Nydia Bruce Daniel

DE GOOD OLE DAYS

"Hummuch fun dem mango todeh,
Miss Maybell?" "Tree fuh cent,
Dem ah de las four pan me tray
Tek dem, me guh content!"

"Miss Janey, eny soursop?"
"Yes chile, dem big an sweet,
Tek paper an rap dis one up
Fuh tuppence" (What ah treat!)

"Miss Flo, me come fuh buy orange."
"Pick out weh pleese yuh Tant —
Ah shillin? Heh, look tenpence change
Since twelve is all yuh want."

(Penny fuh papaya weh sun-bun?
Me lard, Miss Gertie mard!)
"Me change me mine, me nuh wah none!"
She look like she head bard!

She Tootsie gettin up-an-up
Since she get weddin ring,
She sellin farine cent eh cup!
Me lef she wid she ting!

"Ti Sarah, suh yuh plum tree ripe,
Hummuch fuh cal'bash full?"
"Me evva sell yuh? Nuh tark tripe
Shake dong yuh belly full!"

Such was the dialogue we knew
Back in the good old days,
When rice was 'two fuh tree' and 'two
Fuh five' on Saturdays;
When 'salfish bin ah shingle',
And 'hag poke bin ah floore',
When fiddle, bow and 'tengle'
Brought Christmas to each door,
When 'kittle' drum and tambourine
Did never cease to play
So compere, mac'mere, ma deveen
Could dance the night away.

WORDS OF WISDOM

Ma Gramma Sarah bin ah seh tuh al ahwe picknie
Dat wen she naybah showin orf she never-see-come-see.
Dat lady wuz a jokey soul! Wen bumshus Tant come dong
From Pembroke she wud seh, "De contry-bookie come to tong!"

Wen anyone ah dem granson away at nite wud steal,
She greet im wid she coc'nut broom an, "Hoo nuh hear guh feel!"
She wag she finger tuh an fro an slam she ole door shut,
Reminin im, "As shoar as day weh sweet goat run e gut!"

Me oncle Joshua seh e nuh guh tek hun low dong wuk,
Buh still e callin evry day fuh curry goat an duck!
Me Gramma seh, "E nyam carn-fish ur leh e stan e grine
Becarse Joshua, e unly gat hi mine an low behine!"

Matilda bring she new tin-cup fuh beg fuh condense milk,
Dat movay-lang ole fowl come wid she tong as smood as silk,
She grinnin, an she skinnin buh Gramma know weat from charf,
She seh, "Gie she de milk picknie, buh all skin teet nuh larf!"

Miss Janey miss she fowl cock an she holler out an seh,
"Hoo evva teef me wite fowl had bes bring am back todeh!"
Me gramma shake she head den watch me wid she knowin smile,
"Ah teef from teef mek Gawd larf an me tuh, me darling chile!"

Ah hi-brong fella tun sixteen ah hole Miss Tiny han,
Me shoar she ole annuf fuh know ah bwoy from ah yong man!
Buh Gramma seh, "Nuh mine she forty picknie, she nuh big,
An after all, dem seh wen hag nuh grow dem call am pig!"

All dem wise ting me Gramma Sarah bin ah tell ahwe,
An doh she kick de bucket livin pass ah century,
Me shoar dem ting she bin ah seh wen happening come about
Wuz fitting, mos' appropriate like yarm fit Joshua mout.

*Note: The dialect in these two poems has been identified by the author
as that of Mornequiton in Tobago, now included in the area known as
Calder Hall Road, and spoken by her grandmother, born in 1844.*

The Region

Nan Peacocke

BELIZE: CENTRAL AMERICA

Carib
Creole
Pania
a green God watches us from a satellite
far above Altun Ha.
Watches
counting down
the ornate timepiece
of a sungod
counting down the centuries
till the moment when
we too
will face
extinction.

The letter falls to the floor with a thud.
Address
Belize Central America
falls with the same thud you hear
when a soldier from her majesty's troops
heaves his duffle bag
to the tarmac at Belize International.
The thud
you hear
through the neighbours' wall
when another Guatemalan peasant
falls from a bayonet
like ripe fruits fall
from an orchard lynching in Gethsemane
and another Congressional Committee
turns its strange movable eyes
in the direction required
by those strategic interests.

Address
Central America
the navel string
between south and north
the fuse
between Homeless and Lord Absentee
between the world's country club
and the waiters
between Superman and his midwife

The letter falls to the floor
of the meeting hall
it is a ship letter from 1797
it is an airletter signed by joint chiefs of staff
it is a message from the Voice of America
via the relay station at Cabo Rojo
In the meantime the planters asked
their agents in London to suggest
that the Garinagu be removed from
Saint Vincent. It is a memorandum
from the governor.
The nib cuts its blue path
across the pages of fine white foam
to Roatan Central America.

There is no city here now
only a stinking monument
Our Lady of Scornful Abandonment.
No country yet
just two old men sitting on the border
at a game of dominoes
shouting in two languages
"Belice es nuestro"

But the land, at least, is free of us
It is not in the hands
that pushed past the limestone curtain
at Placencia
it is free of the hands
that turned the mahogany forest
to cathedral cargos
it is free from the reins held by
buffalo soldiers in the Cayo
riding our ghosts of independence.

And we are innocent.
Ours is not the hand
that wheeled a horse
into Belmopan
in broad daylight.
Ours is not the hand
that slapped to its wooden rump
a bumper sticker for Coca-Cola
the new flag of Belize Central America.
And we are innocent
three sleeping centuries
at the gateway for invasion
watched by a green God.

A Kekchi woman lifts her hand in the meeting hall
lifts her hand from her needle
where she keeps
on cotton strips
the steps
the stitched architecture of skyward pyramids
lifts her hand to speak.

Mahadai Das

THEY CAME IN SHIPS

they came in ships.

From across the seas, they came.
Britain, colonising India, transporting her chains
from Chota Nagpur and the Ganges Plain.

Westwards came the Whitby,
The Hesperus,
the Island-bound Fatel Rozack.

Wooden missions of imperialist design.
Human victims of her Majesty's victory.

They came in fleets.
They came in droves
like cattle
brown like cattle,
eyes limpid, like cattle.

Some came with dreams of milk-and-honey riches,
fleeing famine and death:
dancing girls,
Rajput soldiers, determined, tall,
escaping penalty of pride.
Stolen wives, afraid and despondent,
crossing black waters,
Brahmin, Chammar, alike,
hearts brimful of hope.

I saw them dying at streetcorners, alone, hungry
for a crumb of British bread,
and a healing hand's mighty touch.

I recall my grandfather's haunting gaze;
my eyes sweep over history
to my children, unborn
I recall the piracy of innocence,
light snuffed like a candle in their eyes.

I alone today am alive.
I remember logies, barrackrooms, ranges,
nigga-yards. My grandmother worked in the field.
Honourable mention.

Creole gang, child labour.
Second prize.
I recall Lallabhagie, Leonora's strong children,
and Enmore, bitter, determined.

Remember one-third quota, coolie woman.
Was your blood spilled so I might reject my history —
forget tears among the paddy leaves.

At the horizon's edge, I hear
voices crying in the wind. Cuffy shouting:
'Remember 1763!' — John Smith — 'If I am
a man of God, let me join with suffering.'
Akkarra — ' too had a vision.'

Des Voeux cried,
'I wrote the queen a letter,
for the whimpering of coolies in logies
would not let me rest.'
The cry of coolies echoed round the land.
That came, in droves, at his office door
beseeching him to ease their yoke.

Crosby struck in rage against planters,
in vain. Stripped of rights, he heard
the cry of coolies continue.

Commissioners came,
capital spectacles in British frames
consulting managers about costs of immigration.
The commissioners left, fifty-dollar bounty remained.
Dreams of a cow and endless calves,
and endless reality in chains.

Audre Lorde

COAST MARKET

Hibiscus bright
the sun is rising over Christiansted.

Gouts of plastic litter
along the delicate shoreline
the building shadows lengthen
but the sand is going away
sea corals hauled to build a pier
for cruiseships
a racetrack instead of a Junior High
mud flows from the schoolyard fountains
our seniors fail or emigrate

At sunset
the ginger weeps
for what is growing
and the precious coin
we pay
for making
change.

Martha Tjoe-Nij

SURINAME

Suriname
Your new awareness
as Caribbean Nation
fits like a new dress
that has to be looked at
for the first time
from all angles
A new world
is opening up
Suriname
Putting on her new dress
for Caribbean freedom.

When distance
gave our moon
her magic
Radiating down
Then on the moon
would be like earth
but then the outer way around
thus distance I would rather be
connecting moon and earth
with sound

Joan French

GUYANA

Guyana have everything
Guyana have nothing;
Cows and no milk
Sheep and no mutton
Wood and no new house
Waterfall and no current
Rivers and rivers and rivers
And no water
Sun and no light.

Egg is a luxury
Cheese is out of sight
Gas cylinder join chain gang
Waitin' for a bly;
Next day, next week, next month, who knows?
Why?

Guyana have everyting
Guyana want someting
A big, big, big ting.

Yu goin' try?

Seketi

POEM

Mujercita caribena
Desde las Guyanas alumbrantes
Hasta las aguas infinitas de las mares azules
 Cuantos lenguas sabes hablar!
 Cuantos bailes sabes bailar!
 Cuantos cantos sabes cantar!
Si no son tradicionales
Que sean al menos nacionales
O tal vez regionales
No me presente una opera en una noche de rumba afrocubana
No quiero nada del norte en la tarde de samba bajo el sol
de Brasil
Prefiero un reggae cuando la luna es Jamaiquina
Y necesito un calipso en las calles de Trinidad Tobago
No necesito "Made in England" durante vacaciones en Grenada
Me quitas el "Rock and Roll" cuando huelo lluvias Vicentinas
Mujercita caribena
Baila kawina con la nigra Surinamesa
Canta la Cancion de una Guyanesa
Lucea con la Sudafricana por la solidaridad
Abrasa la Argentina por la fuerte anistad
Ilga hermana a la guerrillera Nicaraguense
Diga Panameno al Canal de Panama
Libertad eterna a la Chilena
Mais para Guatemala para que no sea guatepeor
Mujercita Caribena
Si tus lenguas no sabes hablar
Y tus bailes no sabes bailar, ni tus cantos cantar
Perdoname que te lo digo! Pero asi no vas a triumfar

POEM *(author's translation)*

I prefer a reggae when the moon is Jamaican
And I need a calyso in the streets of Trinidad and Tobago
I don't need made in England during holidays in Grenada
Please stop the rock and roll when I smell Vincentian rains
Sweet Caribbean woman
Dance the kawina with the Surinamese negroes
Sing the song of a Guyanese woman
Struggle with the South African woman in solidarity
Embrace the Argentinian woman in friendship
Say sister to the Nicaraguan guerrilla woman
Say Panamanian to the Panama Canal
Eternal freedom to the Chilean woman
Born for Guate'mala' not to become Guate 'worse'
Sweet Caribbean woman
If your tongues you cannot speak
And your dances you cannot dance; or your songs sing
Excuse me for telling you! But you won't be victorious so

Olive Senior

COLONIAL GIRLS SCHOOL

for Marlene Smith MacLeish

Borrowed images
willed our skins pale
muffled our laughter
lowered our voices
let out our hems
denied our sex in gym tunics and bloomers
harnessed our voices to madrigals
and genteel airs
yoked our minds to declensions in Latin
and the language of Shakespeare

Told us nothing about ourselves
There was nothing about us at all

How those pale northern eyes and
aristocratic whispers once erased us

How our loudness, our laughter
debased us

There was nothing left of ourselves
Nothing about us at all

Studying: History Ancient and Modern
Kings and Queens of England
Steppes of Russia
Wheatfields of Canada

There was nothing of our landscape there
Nothing about us at all

Marcus Garvey turned twice in his grave.
'Thirty-eight was a beacon. A flame,
They were talking of desegregation
in Little Rock, Arkansas. Lumumba
and the Congo. To us: mumbo-jumbo.
We had read Vachel Lindsay's
vision on the jungle

Feeling nothing about ourselves
There was nothing about us at all

Months, years, a childhood memorising
Latin declensions
(For our language
— 'bad talking' —
detentions)
Finding nothing about us there
Nothing about us at all

So, friend of my childhood years
One day we'll talk about
How the mirror broke
Who kissed us awake
Who let Anansi from his bag

For isn't it strange how
northern eyes
in the brighter world before us now

Pale?

Rumeena

EEN JAAR REVOLUTIE

duiven
duiven van vrede
jammer genoeg geen maretak
een fajalobi
liefde
vurige liefde
in de schaduw van de onderdrukking
de schaduw ook
van de revolutie
de strijd om het recht
de slachtoffers
in het *rood* van hun bloed
tussen het *groen* van de vruchtbaarheid
en het *geel* van de eenheid
die tot uiting komt
in het *wit* van de vrede
waar ze voor vochten
met de Uzi
teken van vrijheid
vrijheid en rechtvaardigheid
voor het volk
van Sranang

ONE YEAR OF REVOLUTION

doves
doves of peace
alas no mistletoe
a fayalobi
love
ardent love
in the shadow of the oppression
the shadow too
of the revolution
the struggle for justice
the victims
in the *red* of their blood
between the *green* of the fertility
and the *yellow* of unity
expressing itself

in the *white* of the peace
they fought for
with the UZI
symbol of liberty
liberty and justice
for the people
of Sranang

Marguerite Wyke

A BASIN OR A CAGE?

> *"...upon the watery plain*
> *The wrecks are all thy deed..."*
> Byron

Bartered and stolen by kingdoms and republics,
these once-plundered islands of sand and palmsticks
we so confidently illume
cannot possibly be immune
to the infection the Caribbean knows
is virulence from every treaty's prose.

Everything we own is here
in this hook of planisphere,
sun-burnished and reconceived
in our self-image and love-leaved.

A be-muddled, aged French general bellowed "dust specks",
A northern republic behaved as if insects
were worrying their capacious pockets.
The least-loved are constantly betrayed
by the huge unsalvaged and decayed;
but they are aware of the depravities
lodged in the sights of their knowing navies.

The hurricane has no effrontery
Obscene as their rockets
souring our sea.

This sea, lane for galleons with black gold was a grave
for island-despoilers, encasing knave,
buccaneer and pillagers from many proud
predatory countries in its sargasso shroud.
Today no barnacles will ever encrest
The new conquistadors aligned with the West,
Their highways are jet-stapled skyways
and cynical, brittle, verbal highways.

Colossus owns the compass, in his groins
is a working knowledge of guile and ruins.
We survivors who know how much it mattered
that our ancestors' flesh and blood were spattered
in that monstrous orgy of servitudes,
fear that behind unctuous, self-righteous platitudes
there's a savage purpose with a savage tool
dredging the same old chains from the slimed pool.

The conquered cities that burned under Rome's spell,
learned to function near Philistia but saw hell
to preserve their crystal countenance intact
within a spacious insouciance. They would act
in a mock
playlet designed for sentient but impotent seers
to appease the Roman consuls and their peers.
But no cries from the wilderness of a bludgeoned heart
will ever deflagrate the generals' specious art.
Can a rock
be foiled by fungus? Do we, perennially alien,
confronting Colossus with Daedalian
artifice from the womb of our woven shell
believe that these puny oscillating waves
will wash his nuclear stones from their barbarous caves?

MADNESS WAS THEIR IDEOLOGY

(A memoir of British Guiana)

Madness was their ideology
compounding the terror of their secret words
encased in self-myth and suddenly
that sullen southern colony
became another foul lair
all guilessly entered except the few
conscience-clothed sifting dust from ground-shock
lascivious as a nude volcano
scumbling the ochre sky
and crying tears of stone.

And so another country lay prone,
its heartstrings severed by a book
become a brutal legend adrift between
the brittle thrust of belief and massive
intrigue assymetrical against the vastness
of umber rain and raw sienna.

Did the CIA devise their ritual
scavenged from some dark-whelmed monstrous plan
which subsidised the bath of blood,
gouged out their native land with British guns,
pitted race against race and slew their sons;
or did a cretin tell them what to do
in words mouthed through a cretin's spittle?

Everything in this taupe dismembered land
was alien to those stunted men roaring
their acrid idioms through countries
being delivered by the forged free, self-sprung
from canefields and paddies and the soucouyant
in the mind.

But where, O where beneath that shadowed
ambivalence lay the sanitary sanity
searching out the human and the innocent
chaste, unpreyed upon, unmutilated
by the scarred stars? But have they shaken
those maggots from their hair and ceased crying
holy on their burdened bones?
And have they cried the final unconniving
word of Guyana's self-hood and dissolved
that madness, its death-scale,
its cruelly contaminating stones?

Evelyne

CARIBBEAN CREATION

Watch them
these two
glide near
so different
exotica
a bloom of genes
grown from
many strains
sharp Angles
erased by supple Asia
velvet skin of Africa
stretched tight
grace of the gazelle
strength of the lion
lush mouth
flashing smile
eyes of brown
amber flecked
slim, tall and straight
as the sugar cane
passionate as the fire
that burnt the cane
their ancestors planted
watch them dance
with the strength
and verve
and joy
of the New People
from the blue waters
and waving sugar cane
of the sun drenched
Caribbean Islands.

Pauline Melville

BATHSHEBA AND ORLANDA

It was something about those shell-thin china cups,
Bathsheba,
Their swimming glaze of blue
That changes with the light,
Their salmon pink exterior, awash with dreams,
Their fine black rims,
That introduced me
To the delicacy of your nature.

True to Caribbean history,
You work to weave together differences,
Driving through canefields
Listening to Bach cello suites
Played by a Japanse musician.
And after long years
Of integrity and committees,
Your smile returned.
Sunshine burst out
Like the yellow allamanda.
Your brown brow was smoothed.

It was something about the silver apostle spoons,
Orlanda,
Their tiny, exquisite scoops, fashioned for honey,
Their slender stems of twisted filigree,
Each branching out to clasp
An opaque stone of shifting mystery,
That let me understand
The fine metal of your nature.

At night your spirit rides horseback
Over Cuba's Oriente
And along the white beaches of Barbados
Scattering poems
Like fireflies over the almond tree.
After so much uncertainty,
You stand laughing
In that deep blue cotton kimono
With its lush undergrowth
Of pagodas, pink peonies
And fresh green foliage.

Clearly, the cups and spoons
Belong in the same house
Where the white jasmine
And the mahogany
Grow together in the yard.

Louise Bennett

DUTTY TOUGH (THE GROUND IS HARD)

*"Rain a-fall but dutty tuff": wages rise but so do prices
and the cost of living.*

Sun a-shine but tings noh bright,
Doah pot a-bwile, bickle noh nuff,
River flood but water scarce yaw,
Rain a-fall but dutty tuff!

Tings so bad, dat now-a-days wen
Yuh ask smaddy how dem do,
Dem fraid yuh teck i tell dem back
So dem noh answer yuh!

Noh care omuch we dah-work fa
Hard time still eena we shut,
We dah-fight, Hard-Time a-beat we,
Dem might raise we wages but —

One poun gawn awn pon we pay, an
We noh feel noh merriment,
For ten poun gawn on pon we food
An ten poun on we rent!

Salfish gawn up! mackerel gawn up!
Pork an beef gawn up same way,
An wen rice an butter ready,
Dem jus go pon holiday!

Cloth, boot, pin an needle gawn up,
Ice, bread, taxes, wata-rate!
Kersene ile, gasolene, gawn up
An de poun devaluate!

De price o bread gawn up so high
Dat we haffe agree,
Fe cut we y'eye pon bread an all
Tun dumplin refugee!

An all dem mawga smaddy weh
Dah-gawn like fat is sin,
All dem deh weh dah-fas' wid me,
Ah lef dem to dumplin!

Sun a-shine an pot a-bwile, but
Tings noh bright, bickle noh nuff!
Rain a-fall, river dah-flood, but
Wata scarce an dutty tuff!

Opal Palmer Adisa

ATTACK AT DAWN*

These are dangerous times.

There is no one within reach.

I am too far
away from home.

I am a slave
my mother is a slave.
This is the law of
the land.

The man who fathered me
is a tyrant
his rape of my mother
is celebrated.
This is the law
of the land.
I am holding
my breath;
my chest cracks and crumbles
under the strain.
All my blood

is drained.
They have killed
my boy.
Maurice Bishop is dead.
Dead.
Dead.
Suddenly,
the meaning of my name
is a task.
The market is empty.
They have killed my boy.
Maurice Bishop is dead.
Dead!
Dead!

The yearning
for my name to pave roads,
water nutmeg
is brushed aside
like some idle fly.
My boy is dead.
I am a slave.
This is the law of
the land.

There must be another word,
synonym
for pawn,
imperialism,
capitalism,
communism,
democracy.

Maurice
a man
helping us believe
we could govern
our own lives.

These are dangerous times.
I let out my breath:
sweat, splinter and bones
scrape my mouth.

My boy is dead.
Once more
we are roped
and battered.

*Attack at dawn refers to the invasion of Grenada
by U.S. troops on October 25, 1983.*

Grace Nobbee-Eccles

THE DURATION IN TRINIDAD AND TOBAGO: WORLD WAR II

This Trinidad before the War
Was a nice quiet place,
It was a haven for all folks
Of every creed and race,
I had a lot of time to stand
A lot more time to stare,
My cup of boredom was quite full
My cupboard never bare.
The Germans started World War Two,
By invading small Poland
And Poland's S.O.S. was answered
By armies in England.
At that time we were British folk
Under her domination
And she defended our shores
Aided by Americans.

Winston Churchill, Theodore Roosevelt
Great Statesman of my time,
Met in the mid Atlantic
Some strategy to design
To save the British colonies
From war and mass destruction,
An incidentally save us
From foreign domination.

Prime Minister and President
Mapped out a plan on paper,
Signed on the wild Atlantic called
The Great Atlantic Charter.
They set out terms and conditions
Restricted areas,
And leased a portion of our land
The Western Peninsula
Air planes just bursting at the seams
Brought scores of Americans
This may be well and truly called
The Great U.S. Connection
Naval bases rose overnight,
Work was offered to all,
We worked like Trojans in the day,
At night we had a ball.
We spanned rivers, diverted streams
Bulldozed hills, filled up holes
And built a tree lined corridor
With huge electric poles,
The Crown acquired private lands
Connecting East and West,
Of all the roads in Trinidad
This was indeed the best.

The Churchill Roosevelt Highway's
The name of this grand road,
During the war it was crammed with
M.P.'s and trucks with loads.
If U.K. or U.S. came now
They'd beat a quick retreat
This road may flaunt a local name
Which may not smell as sweet.
To send a Christmas cake abroad
Required several permits
The cake was prodded, ripped apart
For atom bombs inside it.

I stood in long lines for permits
From which I couldn't escape,
I found myself so often quite
Entangled with red tape.
If I lighted a cigarette
And bent to take a puff,
Sentries would snatch it and exclaim
"It's black-out, that enough."
If I just lingered on the street
To chat with an old friend
Policeman cried 'That's treason
The jail will be your end"

Building materials disappeared,
Housing became acute,
Some avaricious landlords became
More and more astute
They raised their rentals ceiling high,
Demanded huge rewards,
Some tenants lived like chickens, and
Some landlords lived like lords.
Powerful searchlights slowly moved
Turning darkness to light,
They penetrated land sea and
Dark corners of the night.
The convoyed ships far out at sea
Sailed into a safe harbour,
All praise to the courageous crew
Who lived in constant danger.
When friends dropped by we'd gather round
And on the piano lean,
And sing that haunting World War song —
"My own Lilly Marlene."
As war wore on we met no more
We kept our profile low
We could not cope with black-outs and
With transportation woes.

I used to dread the sirens' wail,
And quake through a black-out,
But by degrees my failing heart
Grew very strong and stout.
Whenever I heard the alert sound
I scampered helter skelter,
Grabbed sandbags and elbowed my way
Right through the air raid shelter.
I recollect with hanging head
How coy I used to be,
When gentlemen upon the street
Lifted their hats to me,
But when the Greyhounds sped past
I blew kisses. It was thrilling
To hear whistles, see beck'ning hands —
And scores of "Barkis' Willing".
White collar folks, teachers and clerks,
Discarded ties and collars,
And hurried to the naval base
To harvest U.S. dollars.
They boarded buses, trucks, and jeeps
And worked even at Christmas,
Every street, highway, lane and road
Led straight to Chaguaramas.

My yardboy, chewing gum was now
A fresh water Yankee,
Said "ah working steady with no
Pink slips in sight for me,
Several chains dangled from his neck
He drawled "Don't find it strange
If you buys anything for me
I sez "Joe keep the change".
My cook sobbed "Ma'am Ah hate to leave,
Me heart well sad an sore
It's not because Ah love you less,
But dem Yankees pay more.
I'm now a fulltime housekeeper,
For some American,
It look like all ah dem name Joe.
All call me Mary Ann".

It was quite clear I had to change
My leisurely lifestyle
And do my own housekeeping, shop
And walk mile after mile,
With basket and some paper bags
I went to my old grocer,
I had to bend quite low for he
Now traded 'neath his counter.

I heard the echo of street cries,
From Vendors loud and clear,
Calling out names of things they sold
On streets just every where.
They toted fish, provision fruits
In bags and trays and baskets
But they deserted all the streets
And whispered in black markets.
With vigour I enlisted in
The "Grow More Food" campaign
And chopped down most beautiful trees
To plant peas and plantain.
Sadly enough this whole island
Can't end the wild tree cutting
In parks, savanahs, highways, squares
There's always endless chopping.
For equal distribution we
Were given Ration Cards,
I was just simply forced to stop
My wild desire to hoard.
I stood in queues for frosted cakes
And half an ounce of garlic,
I didn't always need these but
Became a queueaholic.
There was a time I'd rather die
Than peep in shoppers' baskets
But then I pried and owners asked
To show me hidden markets.
I revelled in my legal right
To raise a hue and cry,
And run and tell a policeman
When prices were too high.

Many battles were fought and won,
And War is on the wane,
And all my shopping can be done
By telephone again.
I'm sad to see all purchases
Securely wrapped in paper,
I cannot peep or pinch or know
Who's cooking what for dinner.
V-day has come and Peace again
Settles from shore to shore
And men of faith and of good will
Build on the ruins once more
Lets hope that there will come a time
When nations near and far
Will know "Peace hath her victories,
No less renowned than War.

The now generation may think
This an exaggeration
But they were really not around
During the long duration.
But those who with me faced the War
Through every changing year,
Will vouch for every word I write
We know. For we were there!

Leonie Kessell

TRINIDAD

Tucked in at the end of the red earth road
Is the Hindu temple — plastered, white-washed
Very heathen with its prayer flags planted
In the earth — red and white squares of cotton
At the ends of long bamboo poles — the edges
Frayed by the wind and supplications,
Crowded upon the temple are the Indian workers
Homes — mud ajoupas raised on packed earth
Platforms so the rain will not wash away the walls
These walls sludged with lime and patterned
With children's palm prints in Reckett's blue.

The thatched roof is cool even if it
Sheds the harbouring scorpion and fast centipede.
In the evening the water buffalo is tethered in the grass
Its gentleness belying its sharp horns and heavy
Leathered body. It ploughs the earth for the
Rice farmer and carries his doe-eyed children on its back.
In the town the Indians are more sophisticated.
They suffer the heat of corrugated roofs and
Cement block walls which capture the sun and hold it
Seething, far into the night.
The old grandfather swings away the afternoon
In the sack-cloth hammock strung from the
Pillars which hold the house aloft.
He shares this wind-way with bare-neck fowl
And skinny dog, parts of an old fridge, a rusty
Gear box, a tyre worn to the canvas, a bag
of cement turning to stone and two clay coal pots.

Up there in Laventille live many of the pan men
Clever beaters and ardent suitors of the steel bands
Their black faces gleam in the strung lights of
The pan-yard — muscles strong as they conjure the miracle of
Music from old oil drums. This music penetrates the skin
Enters the walls of the chest, squeezes the heart
Presses down on the lungs then bursts
From every cell's pore.
Today the steel bands are more sophisticated
The ping-pongs and basses, contraltos and altos
Are stacked, two-storied on motorised trucks
The pans amplified and silver chromed.
No more the pushing pan-men at Carnival
On J'Ouvert morning — but it's still
Eyes dulled with fatigue and weed and
A child nine months later. "Don't have
A carnival baby" — but who cares when the
Pans throb in the womb and the loins.

Brooding darkly, over-looking all — when it
Can get its head free of rain clouds, is
El Tucuche — the green, flat-topped peak
In the endless ranges of the north.
Giant earth worms gurgle like suffering
Bellies in the black soil of the high forest paths
They dig in panic of escape at the hunters' footfall.

Below the sister peak, Aripo, are bat caves
And waterfalls. These caves which sheltered army
revolutionaries
Still clutch the bodies of two young divers lost
In its River Styx.
Who now would challenge the Mountain Spirits
Papa Bois, Mama d'Glo, the Soucouyant, the poor Douen
With feet turned backwards, these the unbaptised children
Playing at night in the cold mountain streams
Pulling the claws from the crayfish,
Squealing and jostling and harrying the golden
Furred manicou.

Anybody who is anybody in Trinidad —
And that means the white and done-well-for-himself
Black, the politicians, doctors and lawyers of any colour
Live below the rims of the hills
Mostly on the hot, away-from-the-sea
Flat-land behind the town.
Why should this be? The poor, wanting escape, took
Possession of the heights with breezes and views,
Tight winding roads and land slips.
The rich hid themselves inside walled, watch-dogged gardens
Close to the Savannah where early evening
Perambulations were social occasions to
Proclaim one's station.
Now, the Savannah is more sophisticated.
With traffic blocking the town's veins and
Arteries, capillaries and pores
The grand and proud Savannah is now
The world's largest round-about
But roundabout to where? Onward to a past
Of Conquistador greed of possession, the tyranny of
Desire.

Cornelia Frettlöh

THE SPEECH OF THE SISSEROU

I Sisserou, colourful feathered chronicler of the rain-forest,
I greet you, Waitukubuli, Tall-is-her-body, land of the Caribs,
proud defiant island, fire spitting risen out of the turquoise blue
sea. Still you can hear me, little graceful humming-bird, fou-
fou, you who brought Hiali, He-has-become-bright, he, the
founder of the Carib nation, to his father right up in the moon, a
man with a dirty face. As a reward you got your splendid
feathers and your cap and yet today you see his sons and
daughters defeated and dying.

There, look at them, these men and women, once a proud
feared people, that defied and resisted and today plait baskets
and put them up for sale. Listen to me, all you pronged and
dotted snails, small and big, look out, all you lizards and
iguanas. Still the sound of their names can be heard, Colihaut,
Calibishie and Salibia, but nevertheless it is a dying people.
Columbus didn't conquer them, he, who saw land on a Spanish
sunday: domingo.

Many they saw coming and going until they stayed and
engraved their names in their land: Pointe Michel, Soufriere
and Marigot, Portsmouth, Scotts Head and Hillsborough. They,
the colonists, became many until no more space was left for
those who once had set off from the Orinoco and came to settle
from island to island. Doubtless they banished the Arawaks,
killed the men thus founding their fierce reputation, and yet
took their women as wives, the strange language in their
mouths, became a people of masculine and feminine words, but
nevertheless you see them beaten today, thrown aside, expelled
to a reserve. Take an example from them, agoutis and
manicous, make sure that you don't end up like those, a dying
people.

Hasn't this island got 366 rivers, streams and brooks, one for
every day and one more? The sweetest fruits and rarest berries,
don't they grow here? Mountains, valleys and lakes, don't they
gleam daily under the coloured brightness of the rainbow?

I, Sisserou, ancestor of primitive times, admonisher of the future, watchman over peaks and gullies, I call you, palms, ferns and mosses, trees, bushes and grass. Doubtless hurricanes brought devastation and misery, and yet tins, plastic and too much concrete confuse the mind. Today many eyes are looking northward deceived by a glittering shine. Shall we go and live in the sea like the fish? Once asked a distressed and despoiled people. Today you see them dying, their own language already dead. Barely our forgetfulness remembers, recollects old wisdom and lost art.

I Sisserou, heraldic animal of this island, of an impassable hidden dream, I call you, animals and plants:
Apres Bondie Cest La Ter! After God The Earth!

Amy Nicholas

IN PRAISE OF BELIZE

Tek it from Corozal or tek it from P.G.,
From Benque da di West to any one a dem Cayes,
Dat da eight thousand and odd square miles
full a grass and sand;
    Full wid different faces but we da each one Belizean.

Sometime we tired a wi ears di ring,
Di hear how Belize no worth a ting.
Chu man! Wid all dem beautiful beach and cayes
Yu wahn soon see tourist di swarm in like bees.

And no think dat da all we gat!
What about we Maya Ruin whe name big hat?
And if yu want I go on fu mention one more,
We gat Santa Rita right de da wi back door.

Yes man, ya da fu we Belize.
We betta off than some Belizeans abroad di freeze.
Scarcely any place de betta dan whe we gat,
Over ya the cold no ov'er cold and the heat no over hot.

213

Yu could go East or West or any other route,
Belize no stand like some countries whe we study bout,
River ya, lagoon de, all through fu we blessed land,
Water di de fu use like sand.

How wi Belizean products? dem di improve day by day
Da no true dat, I know, some people wahn say.
But the Toucan match da wahn good example a di lot.
Try it you-self! nowadays when you strike, da him dat.

Down South we gat wahn sight whe we mus' treasure like gold.
Pan di Humming Bird road dem mountains jus' beautiful fu
behold.
Then eena dem hills the sleeping giant him lie down de in peace,
Man! da who else but God could mek wahn beautiful land like
    Belize?

Annette L. Trotman

BARBADOS

My country
is
an exotic mulatto woman
basking in the sun,
tortured by the
caress of an incandescent
sea.

My country's
sounds
of breadfruit falling from a tree,
pounding surf, the constant chatter
of an auto age
and music.

My country
smells
like Sunday lunches, fried flying fish,
French perfumes
and sugar.

My country
tastes
like golden apple tangy,
melting coçonut milk, soursop,
saltfish
My country
exudes
heat of sun, sudden
tropical showers,
splashes of sea spray and
delicate breezes.

My country
is
a sultry wench
looking to the future
through
sun-drenched
sunglasses.........

Jennifer Rahim

HOME

Home is where
shipwrecked crusoes
weary from travelling
through hostile passages
in search of lost
El Doradoes landed.
Believing that salt grains
twinkling in white sand
to be signals of welcome
from a long sought
Golden Mistress
they tried to plant
the flag of ownership,
but the unyielding crevice
of this rock-space-promised —
land would not accept the
pointed staff.

Finding nothing
they gazed seawards for
a sign as fishermen
sometimes do at evening,
nodding knowingly while
mending their nets.
"Fish not biting tonight."
These westerly meditations
produce no coded messages
only salt sea-spray
assaulting their eyes
until they mirror the
bloody remnants of a
sunset massacre.

Blinded, persistent fingers
dug deeper but could not see
how they bled from clawing
at resistant rocks —
could feel the slippery warmth
could feel the pain and not
cry-out but s-m-i-l-e
thinking that they had
penetrated my treasured mines,
and the pain must be their
own giving,
coming, coming home.

STILL BIRTH

Lying in the safe
birth waters of a
Caribbean belly,
these islands beat out
their own rhythms
while they await the
birth signals that
will call them out
into a new beginning,

until
opportunist obstetricians
armed with forceps
invade the sanctity
of womb-space,
clamping iron prisons
around the necks of
unarmed innocents,
forcing labour pains
that yanked them into
a civilization
not their own
not their time
not their way.

The pain of artifical
labour stretches through
drum rolls of time,
while this unwanted
surrogate mother-land
squeezes sugar-labour
and life out of the blood
and sweat of islanders.

And this Mother crying
for her children,
still feels the cold
steel grip tearing the
life from her womb
as the forceps change
into the hands of children
who bear the triple six
seal that reads:
Duvalier, Batista, Burnham.

She's waiting, this Mother
in her secret knowing
for the right moonface
and tide that will begin
the birthing of her
island children
in their own time
in their own way.

Haiti,
the contractions begin
the water bag bursts
crying freedom
Cuba,
the movement down
the passageway
taking deep breaths
the pain sharper, faster
Grenada,
we coming
reaching for the door
that will end one journey
and begin another.
Anticipating the life—
cry the Mother searches
her brain for a name...
Walter
Maurice

We still waiting.

Sita Parsan

MAMA SRANAN

Uit alle windstreken
kwamen zij
om voor ons
een paradijs
te bouwen.

Armoede,
honger en
pijn
hebben zij gekend
om ons.

Verwend
dat wij zijn
hebben wij
alleen maar geoogst
en de opbrengsten
veilig gesteld
in alle windstreken

Uit hebzucht
en luiheid
gaven wij
niets terug
aan ons
paradijs.

Mama Sranan
je bent
uitgeput
en bloedt
dood.
Kom,
laten wij
jou
in veiligheid
brengen.

Uit dankbaarheid
voor hen
die kwamen —
voor ons,
en die nog
komen zullen.

MAMA SRANAN

From all points of the compass
they came
... for us
a paradise
to build.

Poverty,
hunger and
pain
have they known
... for us.
Spoilt
as we are
have we
only harvested.
The proceeds
safely put
in all points of the compass.

Out of greed
and laziness
we gave
back nothing
to our
paradise.

Mother Sranan
exhausted
you are
and bleeding
dead.

Come,
let us lead you
let us lead you to
safety.

From gratitude
for those
who came —
for us,
and those
to come.

Dorothy Wong Loi Sing

BAAP-NEMESTHE REGGAE SONG

Baap, nemesthe,
Maam, nemesthe,
Widya says when she is
coming home from school.
Bhai, kaha?
Aaaaaah, nana!
Oooh, accha!
That's fine....

I saw and heard
such a crazy thing
coming home by bus,
Maam,
there was a young Black girl
with snakes in her hair
and a little Chinese drum:
Rom — tie tum!

She was drumming all the way
from home to school
— What a fool! —
Said she had a message
to all of us:
tom — ta tom
playing on her drum
She said
the Time had come
—bom-ba-bom—
to bring all the peoples to Unity
in the whole wide world.
Young and Old
so she told,

of all kinds of races,
of all kinds of tongues,
of all kinds of colors,
ta-ta-tam-tam—

She cried out loud!
'Wooooey! Follow me please,
and sing, and shout,

and spread the News,
like Me!'

You know what's strange, Maam?
She could speak all tongues!
Hindi, Sarnami, Sranan,
Turkish, Dutch, and a bit from Japan,
Russian, Bahasa Indonesia, Chinese, African
languages, even the secret religious ones!
She could sing in Spanish too
and in Antillean Papiamentu.

German, French, Swedish,
Moroccan tongues, more that I can
count or know about
(being only fifteen years old)
So little Widya told
her parents.
She became a little insecure
and asked: 'Can it be true?
Maam? Baap?'

'Accha, larki,
that's real good news!
We're sure it's true!
It will be true!
It's good, it's good!
Accha!'

Y se quedaran los pajaros, cantando....
and birds were singing heavenly
to you and me
everywhere on this tiny planet Earth.

Norma Nichols

INDIAN PROVERBS

JAISA VAYA WAISA GAYA

Utna paaw pasaaryyay jitnee chaddar hoyay
Avsar ko haath say na gawaawo
Elaai say Bachaaw acha
Apnee ijjat apnay haath.

Jab tak saana tab tak aas:
Is haath day us hath lay
Duwidha may dono gayay maaya milee na Raam
Doodh ka doodh panee ka panee.

IT GOES AS IT COMES

Spread your feet as far as the sheet can cover them,
Don't let opportunity pass from your hand;
Carefulness is better than medicine
Your self respect is in your own hands!

As long as there is breath, there is hope:
You give with this hand and receive with the other.
When in doubt you get neither wealth nor God,
Milk is milk and water is water!

JAISEE KARNEE WAISEE BHARNEE

Lakree kay bal bandar nachay
Jaisa desh waisa bhesh
Jaisa karnee waisee bharnee
Kaam pyaara hota hai chaam nahee.

Ghar kee aadhee bhalee baahar saaree nahee
Chaar din kee chaandnee phir andhayree raat.
Apnee galee main kutta bhee shair hota hain.
Jo garajtay hai way barastay nahee.

ONE SUFFERS ACCORDING TO HIS DEEDS

The monkey dances with the aid of a stick!
Change your appearance according to the country you are in!
According to your deeds you will be repaid,
The work that a person does is what is likeable and not his skin!

One half in the home is better than a whole elsewhere.
After four days of brightness, the dark night comes again.
On his own road a dog is a lion
When the thunder makes a noise it does not rain.

Indrani Rampersad

THE PEOPLE OF THE SUGARCANE

(Dedicated to the Hindus of the Caribbean whose ancestry is linked to the sugar cane fields of the Caribbean)

Cold winds
Strong winds
Impending hurricane
For the people of the sugarcane

A suppressed people!
An oppressed people!
Awake!
And activate!

Impotent apathy
Feeds your expression strait-jacketed
To bloom not
To be doomed
To eternal internal exile

Seen but not served
My society
That brought me forth
In false reality

Dance
but let not your bells
reach the ear

Sing
but let not
your tune, your language, your rhythm
disturb

Be free
But let not your freedom
empower you true

You are too loud
Stifled whispers
dissipate through
cracks in corners
and airpockets in carpets

O People of the Sugarcane
How you suffer!
Few care
To grant you rightful admit

You dance the false dance
You sing the false song
Denied to be
Yourself! Your Psyche!

Will you grow tall
and stately as the sugarcane?
To flower in majesty
In the wind of change?

Or will each harvest
Successively breed
Decreasingly stunted ratoons
Of a virility lost
Of a culture lost
Of a Will lost
In a horizon painted Hopeless?

I weep
For the people of the sugarcane!
The dawn of awareness is painfully slow
I fear: Will it be too late?

Phyllis Allfrey

LOVE FOR AN ISLAND

Love for an island is the sternest passion:
pulsing beyond the blood through roots and loam
it overflows the boundary of bedrooms
and courses past the fragile walls of home.

Those nourished on the sap and milk of beauty
(born in its landsight) trembled like a tree
at the first footfall of the dread usurper —
a carpet-bagging mediocrity.

Theirs is no mild attachment, but rapacious
craving for a possession rude and whole;
lovers of islands drive their stake, prospecting
to run the flag of ego up the pole,

sink on the tented ground, hot under azure:
plunge in the heat of earth and smell the stars
of the incredible vales. At night, triumphant,
they lift their eyes to Venus and to Mars.

Their passion drives them to perpetuation:
they dig, they plant, they build and they aspire
to the eternal landmark; when they die
the forest covers up their set desire,

Salesmen and termites occupy their dwellings,
their legendary politics decay.
Yet they achieve an ultimate memorial:
they blend their flesh with the beloved clay.

Nancy Morejón

FAREWELL

Bajo el camino ciertamente enlutado.
allá al final del último sendero,
el jamaicano teje hoy su esperanza.
Quiere que el sol sea nuevo como una
nueva vida.
Su quehacer fue constante.
Tan sólo comparable al anónimo
constructor de la pirámides.
Desbrozó el monte de Kingstontown.
Limó las verandas de la aldea con su
propia miseria.
Miró a las cadenas de montañas
y se dió cuenta de que Jamaica era una isla
sumamente pequeña.
¿Añorar Cuba? ¿Rememorar Haití?
No, campesino, antillano malabarista del sudor,
no has de inmigrar ya más a tus tierras hermanas
para la zafra hórrida y la huelga.
Vuelve tu espalda y continúa fundando el
camino mejor para tu isla.
Di adiós, un a diós jamaicano.

FAREWELL

Along that road of so much suffering —
there, nearing the final bend,
a Jamaican weaves his hope today.
He wants the sun to be new, like a new life.
His task was constant.
Comparable only to the anonymous builder of the pyramids.
He cleared the slopes of Kingstontown,
polished the town's verandas with his own misery,
saw mountain chains
and realized that Jamaica was above all a small island.
Long for Cuba? Be nostalgic for Haiti?
No, campesino, Antillean juggler of sweat,
you need emigrate no more to your sister islands
for the horrid harvest and the strike.

Turn your back and go on building the better way
for your island.
Say farewell, a Jamaican farewell.

The Worker

Audre Lorde

PRODUCTION

One hundred thousand bees
a sturdy hive   ready
three days after the moon is full
we cut honey.
Our hot knives slice the caps of wax
from each heavy frame
rich and pollened
darkness   drips
from the laden combs.

Sadiq loads the extractor
Curtis hums as he hangs on
levelling the spin.
Sweet creeps like bees
through each crack of hot air
Outside the honey house
hungry drones cluster
low-voiced   steady
We strain laughing
drunk with honey.

Before twilight
rows of filled bottles wait
labeled waiting.

It's hard work
making a living
two dollars at a time.

Members of Frome Cultural Club

COLLECTIVE POEM

Cracked hands
Drop down hands
Big hands
Pain Tek over
The hands are very stiff
Rough Hands
Swell hands
Working hands
Nervous hands

Hard working woman
The hands dem corn up
Sick and tired

Dropping the fertilizer has caused
The hands to sore

Hard work mek the hands rough
Dem swell; dem have Artritis
Finger dem swivel up
Finger dem swell

Through di hard work, fertilizer
Mek di hands dem rough
Old age tek place with the hands
Using the bill, the hands corn up
Finger dem seize up
The joints dem numb and shaky,
Pressure cause dat
Years of exploitation takes the poor

These two hands do a lot of work
These two hands yah do a lot of work

Rajandhye Ramkissoon-Chen

MEMORIES OF A GRASSCUTTER

Head tied with rags of cloth
Bare-backed with sweat-shine
Beneath the sun —
That's how my father toiled
My father's father, and his
Cutlassing with the dance of twigs
To the music of the wind,
And beneath the open sky they lay
Counting its jewels for their wealth.
Now, like that old palm-tree stooped
With leaves of withered brown
I long
To hear again the cutlass sounds —
Swish on grass
Knock on root-wood
Clang on vagrant stone
In the fields,
As I lean on the 'crook'd stick'
With the figure-head of my toll.

Joyce Peters-McKenzie

DE RACKET BAR

Me want fo open Racket Bar,
Me hear it mek hardough,
But Veeny say me ha fo tes'
De feasability.

Me aint no marketin' expert,
Me aint pass mats nor stats,
Me can't afford consultants' fee
Me poor like parson mice.

So me go ha fo use me eye
Fo do market survey,
Cause sense mek before book conceive,
De small man glad fo dat.

No overheads, jis underheads,
No income tax returns,
No big signpos' fo draw de crowd,
Jis crookedness an' tact.

Me tink ganja is startin' pint,
Me leeward frien' dream so,
An' den me could diversify
Wid cocaine an' de res'.

Me can't lef' out de contraban'
An' bootliquor from KEYS,
An' den me operate Queen Show
In stocious racket style.

De sidewalk games don't intris me
But U.S. visa do,
Me tink me better check Tall Boy
Fo get legal advice.

Me wish me fine one Spanish Jar!
Me woulda buy Youlou,
Cause dem ole people hoard nuff bread
Fo mek orwee live high.

De police can't ketch-up wid me
Cause fo me little trade
Does retail fo de M.I.A,
An' dem big man don't joke.

Darlin', dis is a crooked worl',
An' if you don't conform
You boun' fo en'up a' poor home
An' Bun Pan res' yo soul.

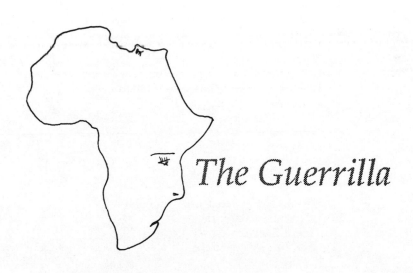

The Guerrilla

Amryl Johnson

MIDNIGHT WITHOUT PITY

Judas
take my hand
let us go from here
down into the valley
keep your hood tight
about your neck
I do not want to see
your face
and if you still remember
the bitter taste
to know
you never stood a chance
or had a choice
against a destiny
which held you
manipulated you
rejected you
then teach me
teach me
teach me how
to count the silver
and forget the cost
for I am
Black
and I am
Angry
My name
is Midnight
without
Pity

Janet Jagan

**TO ALICE, ALSO KNOWN AS KOWSILLIA,
WHO DIED AT LEONORA**

Alice the brave
Alice the courageous
Alice the heroic

Your body
Mangled, ripped
crushed
By the cruel machine
Owned by a cruel
system

The machine
Crushed out your life
As a foot destroys an
ant
As a wheel rolls over
A baby lamb.

Alice, your simple
courage
Defied the outrages
Of an iniquitous system;
Alice, you protested
with your life
Against the inequalities
Around you.

We walked behind your
poor broken body,
Eating the red dust of
the road;
Hearing the angry
rumbling
of an angry people.
Horrified, shocked by
the heartless system
Which crushed the
prostrated body
Of you our Kowsillia
Who said with your
life —
"THEY SHALL NOT PASS".

TO MICHAEL FORDE, WHO LOST HIS LIFE DEFENDING FREEDOM HOUSE

Death did not find you unprepared.
Death did not creep upon you unaware.

You strode with the package of death
Like a soldier; Like the hero you always were.
Your heroism began
Not on that dark Friday of death.
But on the day you understood
And became a revolutionary
To the depths of your soul
To the marrow of your bones.
No fear was in your eyes
No chill went through your body
When you took that death packet
And saved your comrades.
The parson who prayed
over your charred torn body
was apologetic.
Those who murdered you
laughed
When your lacerated body passed by.
But we who love you are not apologetic.

We are proud that men like you
Are born from our struggle
And we will still their laughter,
Yes, their laughter will be no more.

Vanda Radzik

LINGUISTICS #5,
RECKONINGS

You say lines of time like grain of wood
rhyme the rhythm of your life:
This is your content you reason
and remark the pause I make, offering the handle of a knife
I know you will not take.

Well then, how do you find this season?
Which sign carved in tree,
made in mud, stone cast, hand print
will give pause to the indifference of the moving finger,
or reveal an issue of blood?

Which is the colour of ink that counts
And how I ask is a people named
Whose mark is never reckoned?

Jean Binta Breeze

ARISING

(for youths of Azania)

mi madda did fine
wid a likkle roots wine
jus a satta like a vine
pon a tree trunk
while mi faada
young an cute
did jus a play im bamboo flute
an watch im likkle yout
learn fi run

an den dem shatta it

now it come een like a dream
mongs mi people dem scream

an dem sen mi gawn a mission
fi get a education
an teacha bus mi finga
wid a ruler
every time mi ask er bout a
schola-
ship
free passage troo de oceans of time
ah did waan come check out dem mind
fi see how dem conquer troo crime
but
teacher sey ah lookin too high
ongle heaven is up in de sky
an wat ah should become
is a farmer

ah sey
but dat is wat mi faada was
an im did happy
till yuh stappi
an yuh suck wi lan dry
an spit eena wi yeye
like is concentration camp yuh waan sen wi

teacher sey
tun to yuh history book
an let me tell yuh bout Captain Cook
so mi step outa de class
before she tek mi tun ass
a fi mi people pon de crass
an bomb a shatta glass
mi madda feel it
mi fadda tek it
an doan teacher sey mi come from de ape
mi mash it in guerrilla style
mi a flash it in guerrilla style
so mi start a posse pon mi likkle corner
wi start as watch-one fi wi likkle area
wi ban all shoppers fi dem products awn yah
wi discipline wi sista an wi bredda
we tun de revolution teacher
an wi warn all de forces of oppression
dat we, de yout, nah go stop till it done
we yout a go fight

wah fi come wi haffi come
so please
no badda sen wi no toy gun
from Santa
fah wi fighting wid de real ting awn yah
dem put wi to de test
an dem fine we nah jest
fighting wid de real ting awn yah
fah

doan mi madda did fine
wid a likkle roots wine
jus a satta like a vine
pon a tree trunk

wen mi fadda
young an cute
did jus play im bamboo flute
an watch im likkle yout
try fi run

an nuh dem shatta it...

Ramabai Espinet

SPIRIT LASH

You cannot provoke the ghosts of the collective ancestors of all our dark races forever, and receive no comeback. A lash is coming from beyond, and the spirits riding that lash (all the swarthy spirits) will show no mercy as you, the real spooks: colour of bone-ash and driftwood bleached for centuries in an aging sun, fall before their wrath. We call such force a spirit lash.

When a hawk beats
His dying wings into a vermilion
Sun — once gold and flaming
And carries rainless eyes
Yellow with rage
Into his final uncaring
And cats' eyes weep
Dogs' days burn hollow...

Dread the hillsides
Dreadful too the scorched
Sea-lashed earth
Holding no grace but salt

In such dread times
Of sallow sea-fever curses
Yellow rime and quicksand
An eagle — bald and riven
With curses of a thousand
Griefs,
With old contradictions
Choked upon but swallowed whole,
Random, uneven calculations
Of destiny
Now becoming manifest

A bald eagle
Forever distanced
From breaking into BEING,
And no righteous man
No grace
No song unsung...
His haunted visions
Sweetening the breathing cadences
Of the winds of war, volleys
From the battle for love
Of a precious familiar clay
(and now being fought at a cellular level,
with germs, sickle-cell splicing, mosquitoes,
napalm, pesticides, ddt, micro-chips,
food chains, gene pools, eco-systems,
plain and simple misfortune,
and other unimaginable evils)
A clay almost gone sour,
No grace
Not even salt

Only a schoolboy's coarse and
Lecherous fancies for the moon and sun
And all eternal desire
Crammed into his puff-fished face,
While the whole staggering world
Creeps on —
Myopic, unbelieving, grasping at
Every stray tendril of sunlight,
Blinded by fakelights
Christmas tree blinkers
Neon fanlights
And such...

But our dead are with us still.
They do not sleep, unstilled
Like yours whom you fear.
They are not white-coated spooks
Striding through the dark
Haunting the undead
Railing at the unrighteous
Usurping your terrors
And killing your children.

They remain, unaffright,
Sturdy as immortelles
Searching with us for
A world alight with being.
And your still waters,
Now disturbed,
Will die too:
Not so much by eternal
Fire-rage
At Sodom, Gomorrah
Or the Pillar of Salt,
But by slow, blind
Uncaring.

The hawk lashes,
The bald eagle frets,
The seas run together
The dying sun wears down.

Tiffany Robinson

THE LISTLESS WANTON

Pain is felt
It is a long time
It has returned after being
away for so long.

Rejection is seen
It is a long time
She has felt it
It has returned.

Sorrow is heard
from under the seams
of her heart
She is lost within herself.

Love is not heard
It is not felt
It is hidden under the shadows
of the heart.

Listless as it seems
like her
She is the wanton
a bagful of tricks.

Thinking, not knowing
what else to do
This wanton unmasks
herself.

Kindness is lost
time is lost
Feelings are lost
Life is found.

Her face is unmasked
shining through the earth's core
Happy again,
This wanton.................

Lillian Allen

CONDITIONS CRITICAL

Dem a mash it up down inna Jamaica
Dem a add it up down inna Jamaica
Gas prices bounce in hoops for the sky
a little spark and the embers of oppression rise
People tek to the streets. It's *no negotiating stance*
When do you want freedom. *Yesterday*
And how do you propose you'll get it? *By the people's way*
So, that's why, dem a mash it up down inna Jamaica
Dem a add it up inna Jamaica

Dem say dem tired of trying to buy the country back
from the Americans and the IMF pack
A little friendly debt with an open end
and it feels like the ball and chain game again
Conditions critical
Freedom has been mythical
Every few years a new deliverer come
Say: *Better must come, let me lead the way my people*
Seems better get delayed and somewhere hiding
It's quarter to twelve and it's getting late
Better change to waiting and we waiting here a while
and the weight is piling on our backs
And we sweating and dying under disparity's
attacks...attacks
And our children still bawling. And our ancestors
still calling
And we right ya so demanding.

I FIGHT BACK

ITT ALCAN KAISER
Canadian Imperial Bank of Commerce
These are priviledged names in my country
But I AM ILLEGAL HERE

My Children Scream
My Grandmother is dying

I came to Canada
And Found the Doors
Of Opportunities Well Guarded

I Scrub Floors
Serve Backra's Meals on Time
Spend two days working in one
And Twelve Days In a Week

Here I Am In Canada
Bringing Up Someone Else's Child
While Someone Else and Me in Absentee
Bring Up My Own

AND I FIGHT BACK

And Constantly they ask
"Oh Beautiful Tropical Beach
With Coconut Tree and Rum
Why did you Leave There
Why on Earth did you Come?"

AND I SAY:
    For the Same Reasons
    Your Mothers Came

    I FIGHT BACK

    They label me
    Immigrant, Law-breaker, Illegal
    Ah No, Not Mother, Not Worker, Not Fighter

I FIGHT BACK
Like my Sisters Before Me
I FIGHT BACK
I FIGHT BACK.

Dawn Mahalia Riley

DRUM BEAT

*This poem is dedicated to Raquel Candido e Silva, of Brazil;
Hilda Narcisco, of the Philippines; and Anna Chertkova, of the
U.S.S.R. and all others who have been tortured and killed for their
belief in human rights.*

1   The injustice continues
    and while we
    stand and stare
    ten thousand shackles
    bind my sisters in
    the struggle.

2   Time has not erased the pain
    High-handed tyranny
    lives on.
    Far flung is its wretched hand
    to grip, to claw
    your dignity
    our dignity
    woman.

3   The threads of tyranny
    weave their silken strands,
    we are enfolded, entangled
    trapped
    in the mire of
    a no-man's land.

4   We're trapped within
    Fate's cover while
    cries emerge
    from troubled soil
    my breast burns with rage
    Blood turns to ash
    in the midst of the pain
    of an indifferent world.
    Until
    the seed of hope
    bears fruit
    I'll never give up sister...

R.H. Douglas

FIGHT BACK

Fight back!
Don't buckle under
   Fight back!

Open your mouth
Use your voice
No tears should
   be shed
If your ego
   he bruises
       Fight back!

Never let it
   be said
That a Woman
   hides behind
       her tears
          Fight back!

Never let it
   be said
That his flaring
   temper
Gives rise to
   silent rage
       and anger
          expressed only
             in your head.

Shout it out
   Woman
Stand up
   be counted
Womanhood needs you
   Woman
No tears....
   Don't buckle under
       Fight back!

Opal Palmer Adisa

USURPATION

Refusing
to taste
the saliva
of your foul breath
is as valid
as your craving
for flesh
given to you

But when you
plunge
spread raw fire
through me
even after
I scream no
then I want you
annihilated

In Kenya
rape carries
the death penalty

Dawn French

FOR AFRICA

It's a sunny day
And we expected it
Not thankful for it
Expected it.

On the Sabbath
We all dress up and go to church
And on this day of peace
Let's put our hand deeper
In our pocket
And spread some joy
For Africa.

And say a prayer
While you kneel in that pew.

On this beautiful day
As we bathe on a beach
Someone, somewhere
Has no water to drink;
No food to eat

As you think it's not your problem
And a church bell rings again
Think; it calls forth doom
In Africa.

As bellies rumble like thunder
And eyes with death, like lightning flash
And as they dig a tomb;

Dig a little deeper
In that pocket

Pray
Pray a little harder

And as you hear that clock tick

Know
that one more has gone
And six more took his place
In Africa.

Nelcia Robinson

ME A MEK CHANGE

But look on me
trouble
Me get a new name
An agent of change
To help big people change
their behaviour
Imagine! Asking big people to
change their behaviour
And adjust to social change
when you know dem politicians
want to have dem own way
because dem "head in the air"
dem far from reality
An' you know — me have to be
careful
Because me have to earn me
bread and butter!

But more dan dat
Me not trained
Nobody ever tell me how
An me have almost nothing
to work wid
De people me have to work wid
Is who train me
As me bounce me head
me get frustrated
but me learn, and dem
teach and learn as well
Me sure you know what me saying
is true, true, true, — Na true?

So me saying to you
Adult Education
Need new dictionary meaning
somebody wid brain — like Pat
To put together all dem knowledge
dem people have, to mek
sense for me
An we bosses need de same
training like me
So dey could understand and direct we

An yo know something? Me glad me
into educating people
Me really a mek change!

Joan French

FOR ANDAIYE

If you ask me what I remember
It is the wide eyes, head tilted slightly downwards
And behind the ready skin of your face
The humour rising
Through a skin poised not for smiles
But for fighting;
Opening to the lightness of life
To keep the furnaces of anger and of passion burning
As fire feeds on air, but gently glowing.
We have learnt to laugh
Sometimes wryly
but frustration will not surrender;
It creeps around the edges of your curled lips
Rings your smile in circles of cigarette smoke
Feeds your insomnia;
Returns your feet
To the court and the street
The picket and the demonstration beat
And the batons and betrayals of a land of hope gone sour.
Guyana, Guyana, your daughter came home.
Where is her mother?

CAMERA READY

(Original title changed and poem edited for the protection of the innocent.)

I ain' worrin' wid you;
I jus' here goin' about my business
Doin' what I mus' do. An I ain' business
If yu tink a jus' too silent
An' a doan skin up wid certain creature
An' me jeans wash out
An' di hole on di leg want patch up
An' me hair look to you untidy
An' me shirt want changin';
Look how yu want,
I don't care a damn,
I jus' here marchin'
In di ranks of di trying-to-make-it-out-of-oppression
On di road dat will one day lead to liberation
Even if a catch me dead along di way.

I ain' worryin' wid you;
Who matter is dem woman I wid in di jail
Who sing 'Abide wid me' to pass di night
An' when di jailer come to charge disorderly conduct
Tell him to charge dem so dey could go to court
An' tell di judge di officer did charge dem
For worshippin' dey God.

I ain' worryin' wid you;
You ain' see a silent?
A ca'an even bother to waste me breath on you;
I jus' here goin' about my business
I jus' here marchin
Slim, cool, me an me camera....
But di camera not for you....
Is Rookmin I takin',
Rookmin who plant on di back-dam
An wade thru canal an' clear cane
Till her back ben'
For 30c a day.

I ain' business wid you;
Is plenty lick I takin'
When I march in dem march
An' go pon dem demonstration
An' when I go I doan see you
So I doan business wid you;
Is a new Guyana I makin
Wid di family up by Essequibo
No doctor for miles and miles
And mosquitoes and flies
An' disease all roun' dem
An' still fightin';
An' Marlene wid her children belly full o' rice, two peas
An' nutten;
Who still fin' time for organisin'
An' di sister who say she ain' hidin' nutten
Nutten — Burnham was a pig
An' Hoyte ain' no better; is people he foolin'
(People like you);
Is dem I studyin'
So I ain' business wid you;
Step aside;
I passin'.

Bernice Fraser

AN EVENT REMEMBERED

"Ah stap selling!" A slap in the face.
He stood, the boy, not comprehending
Clutching the parent's hand
Who too, is mute with the unexpectedness,
The unfairness of it.
And why should he stop selling?
"Tickets sold from four to six".
Did the print lie?
Fact of black and white betray?
After all these weeks of expectation, preparation?
The careful choice of the nice blue shirt
Marked "helluva kid" had come to this?
The anxious walking, running from long south
To far north had diminished to nothing?

The imagined eye-prints of soldiers
Marching valiantly, making their trumpet
Calls, beating their brisk tattoo, had simply
Dissolved into this overwhelming obstacle of a
shut-fast ticket-booth, a pinioned gate,
Soldiers now that forced back the crowd with
Cruel banded arms, and hearts
More cruel, and banded down by
Callous coldness to the dreams of boys
Who hope still to be soldiers

And there! — the first parachute
Dropping from the sky
Bringing from the sky
Bringing its human burden
Safely to the earth it treads

But the hopes of men skywards fly
Visions do not grow earth-bound
They are born out of the living acts of men
And reach forever upward
Until fashioned in completeness
They descend again
To touch the hearts and lives of men.

Give this boy the food he needs
Vigorous life
Depicted in your play
of simulated signs and scenes.

He too, has a vision.

Sandra Bihari and Angelique Marsan

WIJ, — VROUWEN

Wij, vrouwen
die worden gediscrimineerd,
die worden onderdrukt,
die nooit gelijkheid hebben gekend:
Sta op!
Open je ogen!
Vecht voor gelijke rechten,
die je moeders nooit hebben gekend.
Vecht tegen de ongelijkheid
waarvan wij ooit zullen worden verlost.

Refrein:
Vrouwen,
Sta op!
Doe je ogen open.
Vecht voor je recht.

Vecht tegen hen die zich groot voelen,
Vecht tegen hen die zich machtig voelen.
Vrouwen, kom tot leuvn,
breek de vloek die op je ligt.

Wij, vrouwen
altijd beschouwd als minderwaardigen
altijd pijnlijk opzij geduwd
Vrouwen,
zie de wereld in!
Vecht tegen de discriminatie
die ons zal ruineren.

Refrein:

Wij, vrouwen
die worden onderdrukt,
die worden uitgezonderd;
vrouwen,
Doe je mond open!
En laat die nooit meer dichtsnoeren.
We zullen ons doel bereiken.

WE, WOMEN

(A poem by two secondary school students in Paramaribo)

1
We, women
who are being discriminated,
who are being oppressed,
who have never known equality:
Get up!
Open your eyes!
Fight for equal rights,
which your mothers never knew.
Fight against inequality
from which we will be freed one day.

Repeat:
Women, rise!
Open up your eyes.
Fight for your rights.

Fight against those who feel big,
Fight against those who feel mighty.
Women, come to life, break the curse upon you.

2
We, women
always seen as inferior
always pushed aside painfully,
Women, look out into the world!
Fight against discrimination
which will ruin us.

Repeat:

Women, rise!
Open up your eyes.
Fight for your rights.

Fight against those who feel big,
Fight against those who feel mighty.
Women, come to life, break the curse upon you.

3
We, women
who are being oppressed,
who are singled out;
women,
open up your mouths!
And never let it be shut up again.
We will reach our goal.

Repeat:

Women, rise!
Open up your eyes.
Fight for your rights.

Fight against those who feel big.
Fight against those who feel mighty.
Women, come to life, break the curse upon you.

Claire Harris

LITANY

*For the thing which I greatly feared is come upon me, and that which I
was afraid of is come unto me.*

Job 3. xxvi

Lord it is not a question of what air will accept   we have
seen what it will not   black bodies falling like stones from
forts our planes   heavy silver gulls nose first into seas on
the other hand invaders   are at ease   paratroopers in
current savage with lies   think of them against the wide
Caribbean sky   other things this air will not accept
old wooden houses   freedom   bone   have You
noticed after their bombs   yards away   faintly pink
splinters Lord of the dark grace   tell me what happens the
people cry Lord   Lord   is it rain-stained church walls
that jail poor hope   what do You intend   that this continuous falling: houses/boys/dreams is merely a prelude   tell
me how You will make it up to them   can it be we wear

postures of pain so gracefully Your grief is paralysed in admiration   Once You said   'the meek shall inherit the earth'
Lord of the nutmeg   Lord of the figs   when

Look there   below those shells the air speeds on their way
earth is foaming surf against black sand   in the distance
hammered blue-green sea and islands   You have such an
eye for beauty

Leone Ross

DO YOU HEAR WHAT I HEAR?

This morning I heard a teardrop fall.
I heard it in the house next door.
The baby was hungry and its mother was crying.
I heard it two miles away:
A man's sweetheart left him for money.
I heard it in the next parish:
A child realized he had no comfort.

This afternoon I saw a teardrop fall.
The hungry in Ethiopia
Know that their only hope
Is music
From the throats of the rich.

The blacks in South Africa are hurting
Their women and children want to
leave behind their skins.
The world is like a spinning top
Confusion, war and tears.

Gina Henriquez

YOU ARE NO ORCHIDIST

Why do you want to know
What fragrance is there to you unknown
In the beautiful petals of that attractive orchid
Which perhaps aroused your desire for wanting her

I can tell you so far....
It's better watching an orchid from afar
Than to have her between your finger
Where she cannot linger....

If she's cut from her stem, she'll crush, wither and die
And all you'll have, is a withered flower, a sigh and a cry
So take my advice, leave the blooming orchid
Alone with her joy or her sorrow
And don't try to spoil her bright tomorrow....

Maria C. Diwan

POEM

Mi kreashon
tabata di un repchi
di bo kustía.

No ku parti
di bo serebro
pa hamas bo pensa
ni huzga pami.

No ku parti
di bo kurason,
pa di nos kada un semper
sintimentu ta diferente.

No ku parti
di bo man ni pía,
pa nunka bo maltrata,
oprimi of trapami.

Kreador a trahami
ku'n repchi
di bo kustía.

Pa mustrabo
mi lugá den bida,
kantu di bo.

Pa uní nos lucha,
banda di otro nos logra.
i den amor nos uni.

POEM

I am a woman
creation of a rib
from your side.

How wise the Creator
not to use part of your brain,
giving both men and women
own consciousness and
equal right to think
act and speak.

Neither did HE activate
life in me by the beat
of your heart.
Each one of us controlling
our own emotions and
experiencing different feelings.

Oh man...
While HE created the woman
you were asleep.
You could not use your mind
hands nor feet.
Never abuse, oppress
or trample me down!

I am a creation of a tiny rib
of your strong side.
How wise the Creator...
to clearly show my place in life.
Beside you!

Oh man...
No domination!
Togetherness in achieving goals!
Unification in love!

Ahdri Zhina Mandiela

I AM

i/used to be
a lot of things

now/i am
more

I AM (Part 2) FULL

I am
fully acculturated
a deviant
of your plan
Partial inheritance
you offered
but I stole it all
while you looked on
helplessly
now
you don't recognize me
my foil is impenetrable
more than a mere facsimile
I have detoured
into the difference
becoming now
a legal heir
and the legacy I accept
and shit on it

Nancy Morejón

EN EL PAIS DE VIETNAM

Esta gaviota vuela sobre el eterno cielo de Hanoi,
como antes volaba el agresivo B-52.

¡Qué clara es la ciudad!
Y el reportaje tan lejano hablando de las fiestas
del Tet,
de la victoria popular.

Yo estoy aquí, como una mujer simple,
como hiciera Cheng Urh, como hiciera Cheng Tseh,
para cantar la vida del triunfo
y para levantar, piedra tras piedra:
la escuela y el refugio,
la pagoda de Angkor, las casas de bambú,
la bella arcada de los puentes.

Oh, claro Vietnam, si cae la bomba sobre el mar
lleva tu árbol y tu escudo hasta la puerta del país.
Ciérrala firme.
Y si regresan-no sé, ¿quién sabe? —
sobre el muro de oro,
que el invasor perezca, pérfido, junto al río.

IN THE COUNTRY OF VIETNAM

This sea-gull soars in the eternal sky of Hanoi,
as the aggressive B-52 flew before.

How dazzling is the city!
And the distant report of the celebrations
of Tet,
of the popular victory.

I am here, a simple woman,
like Cheng Urh, like Cheng Tseh,
to sing the life of the triumph
and, stone by stone, to build:
school and bomb shelter,
the pagoda of Angkor, the bamboo houses,
the beautiful arcade of the bridges.

Oh shining Vietnam, if they bomb your sea,
bring your tree and your shield to the door of the country.

Slam it shut.
And if they return — I don't know, who knows?
let the invader perish, perfidious, by the river.

UN MANZANO DE OAKLAND

(para Angela Davis)

¿Ves ese suave y firme manzano
dando sombra sobre una acera gris de Oakland?

¿Lo ves bien?
Cada molécula de su tronco viajó desde los
bosques de Dakota
y el lacrimoso Misuri
Las aguas del gran lago de sal de Utah
regaron las resinas de su corteza.

¿Sabes que ese manzano fue plantado
con la tierra robada a los Rodilla-Herida
por el gobernador del estado?
¿Acaso tú conoces que su savia
se nutre con los huesos y pelos prisioneros
de San Quintin?

Fijate en sus hojas misteriosas,
en los hilillos por donde pasa el jugo de esa savia.

Míralo bien.
Mira bien tú la estación remota que inaugura
Mira bien, niño del occidente norteamericano,
la copa del manzano,
más ancha aún que la misma costa del Pacifico,
la que guarda en su mejor raiz
carabelas y espectros.

Y a ti, viajero, te dará sombra siempre,
pero detén tu marcha pesarosa ante esa sombra suya.
No olvidarás jamás que ha sido
la triste, cruel, umbrosa, la elimera morada
de múltiples cabezas negras colgando entre el follaje,
incorruptibles.

AN OAKLAND APPLE TREE

(for Angela Davis)

See that strong, smooth apple tree
shading a grey sidewalk in Oakland?
Can you see it well?
Each molecule of its trunk has travelled from
Dakota woods and the tearful Missouri.
The great salt lake of Utah
has watered the resins of its bark.

Did you know that apple tree was planted
on land stolen from Wounded Knee
by the governor of the state?
Perhaps you know how its sap
is nourished with the prisoner bones and hair
of San Quentin?

Look hard at its mysterious leaves,
at the tiny threads through which
the juice of that sap flows.
Regard it well.

Observe the remote season it inaugurates.
Observe, child of the Northamerican west,
the apple tree's crown,
broader even than the very coast of the Pacific:
In its great root it keeps caravels and ghosts.

And you, traveller, it will shade you always,
but slow your heavy step before its shadow.
Never will you forget this tree has been
the sad, cruel, shadowy, the ephemeral dwelling
of multitudinous black heads hanging among the foliage,
incorruptible.

Grace Nichols

NANNY

Ashanti Priestess
and giver of charms
earth substance woman
of science
and black fire magic

Maroonic woman
of courage
and blue mountain rises

Standing over the valleys
dressed in purple robes
bracelets of the enemy's teeth
curled around your ankles
in rings of ivory bone

And your voice giving
sound to the Abeng
its death cry chilling
the mountainside
which you inhabit
like a strong pursuing eagle

As you watch the hissing
foaming cauldron
spelling strategies
for the red oppressors' blood
willing them to come
mouthing a new beginning song

Is that you Nanny — Is that you Nanny?

Germaine Y. Horton

CURFEW BREAKER

I thought I'd take a little stroll
As the sun began to set
I walked..and walked until I was told
The curfew wasn't lifted yet

T'was then I realised the time
How could I be so stupidly blind
How could I make such a mistake
As being on the street and almost twenty minutes late.

About I turned and began to count
Five Streets twenty houses I started to run
My feet felt too heavy, My head was in a state
It seemed to me a thousand miles
Before I reached my gate

With relief I sighed on reaching the door
Peep....Peep I heard, who else but the law
'Good night madame!' One gentleman said
The gun in his hand was aimed at my head
'Good night' I mumbled. Can I help you sir?
"Do you know you're breaking the law"
"What" I exclaimed "are you mad"
"Can't one even stand in one's own yard."

Mary Garcia Castro

COMO LEER CINDERELLA EN LATINOAMERICA

(maria gainsville, 1985)

A nosotras nos enseñaron
que deberíamos esperar,
que el grande amor vendría a caballo
bajo uno aureola de luz
envuelto en sonidos graves de trompetas y oboes.

Y nos pusimos a soñar
con el príncipe que debería llegar.

Los amores del día a día eran humanos
sabían a tierra y vivían violencia
y sólo tierra y violencia nos podían ofrecer.

Ojos en el futuro sonado,
dejamos el día a día no gozado.

Evitabamos mirar al lado,
semblar compañeros, hacer tierna
su necesaria violencia,
pues el principe iría llegar.

Para muchas nunca ha llegado
y estas se quedaron en el esperar.

Pero para algunas sí. Para mí sí, un día el llegó
y descubrí, poco a poco
cómo desafinada era su música,
cómo era diferente su país,
cómo eran incómodos los zapatos de vidrio,
cómo su ropa dorada contrastaba con la de mi explotado
pueblo.
Y cómo el era indiferente a las cosas de la tierra,
Y cómo el era violento en su no mirar.

Quería llevarme en su caballo para su país.
Decia que tendriamos esclavos, brillo, dejariamos la tierra
y echaríamos siempre a volar.

Comprendí entonces que a nosotras nos hablaron de príncipes,
pero no de los horrores de la monarquía, del Imperio.
Comprendí entonces porque los compañeros sabían a tierra y
eran violentos. Y cómo podían, con nosotras, venir a ser
tiernamente violentos.
Comprendí entonces por qué el principe sabía a vacío y
era violento. Y como sabía ser friamente violento.

Yo dije no,
Y me resolví quedar.

HOW TO READ CINDERELLA IN LATIN AMERICA

free translation by author

We learnt we should wait.
Our true love would come,
riding a big horse,
enlightned with sunny bright,
and carried by trumpet music

And we dreamt about him,
the prince who would arrive.

Daily love was too human,
tasted earth and violence.
What else besides earth and violence
could we get from them?

We were looking ahead,
dreaming about the future.
And we did not taste the present.

We avoided looking aside,
to sow *compañeros,*
to give tenderness to
their necessary violence.
No, we were awaiting the prince.

For many of us, he never arrived.
These sisters spent their lives, waiting.
But for a few, he did come. Yes, for me,
he arrived.
Little by little, I became aware
how dissonant was his music, how strange was his country,
how the tiny glassy shoes bothered my feet.
How his golden robe was different from the clothes my
poor people had worn..
I became aware how indifferent he was in relation
to earthly things, and how violent he could be,
just not looking around.
He told me stories. He wanted to take me
to his fairy tale country. We would have
slaves, shining clothes, we would be far away from
the earth. We would be flying for ever.

I understood why they told us about the prince,
but never about the horrors of the Empire.
I understood why the *compañeros* were rude and violent.
I understood that we, women, side by side with
them, might transform their violence into tender violence.
I understood why the prince was so empty, and so violent.
And how he could be coldly violent.

I said no, and I stayed.

PROYECTO VIDA

*"te doy una canción como un disparo como un libro, una palabra,
una guerrilla como doy el amor."*

(Silvio Rodriguez)

Este proyecto generado entre líneas,
de negativos, de experiencias vividas a medias,
del más allá, de las sugerencias cogidas del inmediato,
ya no es proyecto.
Este proyecto se hizo pareja,
se hizo hijos, se hizo viajes,
se hizo nieve-y-hierba, y se asustó
cuando se hizo papeles.

A los pocos salió del yo chiquito,
se hizo calles, callampas, prisiones, rumbas, veredas.
Pasó por CentroAmerica nuestra,
descubrió unicornios y caimans en el Caribe.
Subió los montes y se enredó en florestas-fusiles.
Conoció la muerte-laser de la Casa-tumba-Blanca,
y casi se lo compran en un shopping-center de Miami.

Este proyecto se hizo no, y se hizo yo. Un yo
más allá del allá, del aquí, y del ahora.
Del fondo del aquí, del ahora, por el nuevo yo
se hizo compañero-compañera, se hizo multitud.

Cogió la canción, y de la invitación de 'futurar' presentes,
fue 'presentando' futuros.

Este proyecto no es más proyecto,
y mucho nenos una proyección
Se recusó ser papel, más uno proyecto y
se hizo proyectil junto con mil proyectiles, que, en el continente,
disparan futuro en canciones, en versos, en guerrillas, en discur-
sos,
en aciones.

PROJECT LIFE

*"I'm giving you a song, the same way I shoot, I give a book, I say a
word, I make guerrilla war, I make love"*

(Silvio Rodriques)

This project was generated between lines
from negatives, from half lived experiences,
from far away, from suggestions collected from the immediate.
This project is no more a project
It became a couple, it became children, it became trips,
it became snow-and-herb,
and got scared when becoming paper.

Little by little it got rid of the little I,
and it became streets, it became slums, prisons, festivals and
paths.
It went through our Central America,
and discovered unicorns and crocodiles in the Caribbean.
It climbed to the top of the mountains and it got tangled
in rifle-flowers
It met the death in the White-tumb-House,
and it was almost sold out in a shopping center in Miami.

And then, this project became no, and became I.
And I farther away than beyond, farther away than here,
farther away than now.
But from the bottom of here, the bottom of now.
For the new I, it became comrade.
It heard the song, and from the invitation to make the future
present
It went around "presenting futures"

This project is no longer a project,
and furthermore, it is no longer a projection.
It refused to become a paper, to be one more project.

It became a projectile, together with a thousand projectiles, that
in the continent are shooting the future with songs, poems,
guerrilla wars,
with speeches, with action.

Honor Ford-Smith

MESSAGE FROM NI

They write so much of me now
that sometimes I read about myself
(hoping for strength, while I wait
among the piles of empty shoes, the still kisko
carts and the mad mumbling vagrant warriors
in the sidewalk market at Half Way Tree)
I never recognize that woman they describe.
Let me tell you how it really was:
(Like a young tree in a hurricane)
my body shook in battle
I vomited after seeing the dead
and (at first) the smell of blood

made me faint. Blinded by a future
I could not vision, my old words meaningless,
choked to silence in a forest of trees
I had no names for, I fell and fell,
was lost, bled, marooned in a landscape
that grew stranger with each discovery I made.

Once, for hours I climbed that cracked
crumbling black rock, till hunched and
hungry I could stare down at the oceans of cane
bound by the sunlit grid of straight roads
and study the repetitious movements of slaves.
Tied as I am to that treadmill of change,
I envied them obedience's freedom
I hungered for their assured meals
their chance to confuse imitation
with innovation, to trace all evil to
one source outside themselves.

At times like that I cursed the people
they say I led: when the abeng blew
I longed for lovers or children or
invented dreams to fill the hollow
sleepless nights
    (the pumpkin seeds that overnight bore
    fruit to feed us was one, the bullets
    that I caught between my legs and threw
    back at the enemy was another)

I told the others these dreams.
They repeated them. In their believing
I believed myself. That was all I had
to hold against surrender, to hold against
the defeat that would make me visible in
THEIR history and I wanted that,
I was that vain
How I prayed to be freed from what drove
me on: they never mention that, or
how close courage is to fear.
It was terror of terror that drove me on
Till it was all over and I heard
I was Ni
eye of change leadress   path
finder healer of the
breach.

Meiling Jin

THE BOAT GIRL

When I heard about your pain
I wished you dead little girl.

Running from the war, a casualty.
Fleeing the bombardment in a boat.
If only you had died then
My little sister.
Instead of living
To tell the tale.

Seven times it was. Seven times raped.
And thrown into the China Sea.

Nneka

GUNMAN'S PSALM

The gun is I shepherd
I shall always want
He maketh I fe lay down in poverty
He leadeth I to destruction of I onna people
He oppresseth I soul
He leadeth I in de paths of confusion for
politicians sake
Yeah though I send out a hail of bullets
and brutality
I dwell in constant fear of elimination
For cold steel is my comfort and without
him I am powerless
I live off the blood of the working class
and oppressed as a parasite
And when the rite time come
They shall anoint I head with lead
Surely reaction shall always follow I and I
All the days of I existence and
one of these days
Dem will fling I inna grave forever.

The Survivor

Jean Binta Breeze

ORDINARY MAWNING

it wasn't dat de day did 'start out bad
or dat no early mawning dream
did swing mi foot
aff de wrong side of de bed

it wasn't dat de cold floor
mek mi sneeze
an mi nose start run wid misery
wasn't a hangover headache
mawning
or a worry rising mawning

de sun did a shine same way
an a cool breeze
jus a brush een aff de sea
an de mawning news
was jus de same as ever
two shot dead
truck lick one
Israel still a bruk up
Palestine
an Botha still have de whole world han
twist back a dem

no
it wasn't de day dat start out bad
wasn't even pre m t
or post m t
was jus anadda ordinary get up
get de children ready fi school
mawning
anadda what to cook fah dinna dis evening
mawning
anadda wish me never did breed but Lawd
mi love dem mawning
jus anadda wanda if ah should a
tek up back wid dis man it would a
ease de situation mawning

no
it wasn't no duppy frighten mi
mek mi jump outa mi sleep
eena bad mood
nor no neighbour bring first quarrel
to mi door
wasn't de price rise pon bus fare
an milk an sugar

was jus anadda
same way mawning
anadda clean up de mess
after dem lef mawning
a perfectly ordinary
mawning of a perfectly
ordinary day
trying to see a way
out

so it did hard fi understand
why de ordinary sight of
mi own frock
heng up pon line
wid some clothespin
should a stop mi from do nutten
but jus
bawl

Anielli J. Camrhal

BLUE TARANTULA

(To Dad)

When I was young
Insects were one
Of child's worry
Until the day
Dad told me
Ten thousand
Ten million times
Bigger you
Are
With a smile
Don't you think
They're
Afraid of
You
I accept
That wise
Advice
So when
A few years
Later
Walking along
Les Pitons du Carbet canal
I met a beautiful
But lethal
Blue tarantula
My Dad's secret
Came to my mind
And Lady Spider
Amazed by my quietness
Decided to go on
Her trip...

Jane King Hippolyte

FELLOW TRAVELLER

You hear the rain crossing valley?
You know it will strike us quite soon?
You know how this damn roof is leaking?
Well, of course you must know,
For you holed it yourself
When the wind start to blow
On the day that you said
The damn walls hold you in
And you feel like you dead
And you gone on the roof there, to dance.

You said how you were sure
If you climbed right up high
Felt the sun right above you,
Your hair in the sky,
You would see far far.
That the walls block you up,
That the walls "paw" you in
And you danced and you laughed.

Now, I was afraid you would fall down.
You said No, and, So what if I do?
Is just safety you want?
I have things I must see
And I can't keep on thinking bout you.

But you knew I would stay here inside it.
You knew I would wait here for you.
Now I wait and have waited and will wait
But my dancer, the rain's coming in,
And you see how that big storm is brewing?
Where's my shelter?
I drowning again?

You see you, dancer,
Big smile on your beautiful mouth?
You see you, seeker?
Fix the roof.
Or is I moving out.

Olive Senior

TO THE MADWOMAN IN MY YARD

Lady: please don't throw rocks at my window
because this is Holy House and God sent you
to get all the moneylenders out drive the harlot
from the inner temple. Again. Please don't
creep up behind me when I'm gardening beg me
lend you a knife. A bucket. A rope. Hope. Then
threaten to ignite, set alight and consume me
for you are the Daughter-of-a-Eunuch-and-a-Firefly
sent to X-ray and exhume me.

Lady: this is nonsense. Here I am trying hard
with my Life. With Society. You enter my yard
dressed like furies or bats. Bring right in to me
all the hell I've been trying to escape from.
Thought a Barbican gate could hold in the
maelstrom. Keep out the Dungle. And bats.

What you want? Bring me down to your level?
— A life built on scraps. A fretwork of memory
which is garbage. A jungle of images: parson
and hellfire all that's sustaining. The childhood
a house built of straw could not stand. The man
like a roach on the walls. So you choose
out of doors. Or my garden.

Lady: as you rant and you shout, threaten
and cajole me, seek me out then debar me
you don't move me one blast: Life Equals Control.

Yes. Here is what the difference between us
is about: I wear my madness in. You wear yours out.

Shirley Small

VISIONS OF THE PAST

To lie not sleeping,
drifting into sleep
or drifting out
and see file by,
with eyelids closed,
a real parade of faces
flesh of my flesh
blood of my blood,
I know their anguish and their fire.
Some look sepulchral
Eyes closed, cheeks sunk
Some have gaunt cheeks
but chins of steel
And some flash fire
from defiant eyes
But all are beautiful
and all reach out to touch me as they go
and I know
My sisters and my brothers, all.
Brothers in travail
And I see why
their tortured past
left swells, upheavals
that yet flood our lives.
That mighty tidal sweep
that strives to press us to the floor
is that same force
that took their lives.
But through times' murky waves
we have maintained
soul's primal fins and gills
and so we breathe life's inspiration
and remain
the wonder
that we are.

(with permission of the Congress of Black Women Montreal)

Joy Wilson-Tucker

BEING BLACK

I'm not ashamed of being black.
Who states that I must hide my face
Because my color is a disgrace?
I'm not ashamed of being me
I'm black and very proud to be.
Who states my color should be defined
And I must stand behind the line?
Intermingled color chain
From this no one can refrain
Sister — Brother — Cousin — Friend
All inherit this great land.
Though black, they've no desire to be
Outcasts of society
I'm not ashamed to state my case
And in this Island take my place
To carry on my foreparents-plan
In this trying, bitter land.
Although my color may hinder me
To a certain vast degree
I'm not ashamed of being me
'Cause black is all I care to be.

Amryl Johnson

SHACKLES

The dividing line is slim
It exists no more
Ironic laughter rippled
through the breeze
the night
a leaf
as cold as iron
blew against my feet
clung to my ankle
Shackled dead

in my tracks
catapulted back
in time
to taste
the icy thorns
of sorrow
Sent me stumbling
like a lunatic
to a bar
    Drink up!
the man said
    It's closing time!
I choke
on the dregs
of my ancestry

Nancy Morejón

MUJER NEGRA

Todavía huelo la espuma del mar que me hicieron atravesar.
La noche, no puedo recordarla.
Ni el mismo océano podría recordarla.
Pero no olvido al primer alcatráz que divisé.
Altas, la nubes, como inocentes testigos presenciales.
Acaso no he olvidado ni mi costa perdida, ni mi lengua an-
cestral.
Me dejaron aquí y aquí he vivido.
Y porque trabajé como una bestia,
aqui volví a nacer.
A cuánta epopeya mandinga intente recurrir.

        Me rebelé.

Su merced me compró en una plaza
Bordé la casaca de Su Merced y un hijo macho le parí.
Mi hijo no tuvo nombre.
Y Su Merced murió a manos de un impecable *lord* inglés.

Anduve.

Esta es la tierra donde padecí bocabajos y azotes.
Bogué a lo largo de todos sus ríos.
Bajó su sol sembré, recolecté y las cosechas no comí.
Por casa tuve un barracón.
Yo misma traje piedras para edificarlo,
pero canté al natural compás de los pájaros nacionales.

Me sublevé.

En esta misma tierra toqué la sangre húmeda
y los huesos podridos de muchos otros,
traídos a ella, o no, igual que you.
Ya nunca más imaginé el camino a Guinea.
¿Era a Guinea? ¿A Benin? ¿Era a
Madagascar? ¿O a Cabo Verde?

Trabajé mucho más.

Fundé mejor mi canto milenario y mi esperanza.
Aquí construí mi mundo.

Me fuí al monte.

Mi real independencia fue el palenque
y cabalgué entre las tropas de Maceo.
Sólo un siglo más tarde,
junto a mis descendientes,
desde una azul montaña,

bajé de la Sierra

para acabar con capitales y usureros,
con generales y burgueses.
Ahora soy: sólo hoy tenemos y creamos.
Nada nos es ajeno.
Nuestra la tierra.
Nuestros el mar y el cielo.
Nuestros la magia y la quimera.
Iguales mios, aquí los veo bailar
alrededor del árbol que plantamos para el comunismo.
Su pródiga madera ya resuena.

Nancy Morejón

BLACK WOMAN

I still smell the foam of the sea they made me cross.
The night, I can't remember it.
The ocean itself could not remember that.
But I can't forget the first gull I made out in the distance.
High, the clouds, like innocent eye-witnesses.
Perhaps I haven't forgotten my lost coast,
nor my ancestral language.
They left me here and here I've lived.
And, because I worked like an animal,
here I came to be born.
How many Mandinga epics did I look to for strength.

       I rebelled.

His Worship bought me in a public square.
I embroidered His Worship's coat and bore him a male child.
My son had no name.
And His Worship died at the hands of an impeccable English
lord.

       I walked.

This is the land where I suffered
mouth-in-the-dust and the lash.
I rode the length of all its rivers.
Under its sun I planted seeds, brought in the crops,
but never ate those harvests.
A slave barracks was my house,
built with stones that I hauled myself.
While I sang to the pure beat of native birds.

       I rose up.

In this same land I touched the fresh blood
and decayed bones of many others,
brought to this land or not, the same as I.
I no longer dreamt of the road to Guinea.
Was it to Guinea? Benin?
            To Madagascar?Or Cape Verde?

I worked on and on.

I strengthened the foundations of my millenary song and of my
hope.

I left for the hills.

My real independence was the free slave fort
and I rode with the troops of Maceo.

Only a century later
together with my descendants,
from a blue mountain

I came down from the Sierra

to put an end to capital and usurer,
to generals and to bourgeois.
Now I exist: only today do we own, do we create.
Nothing is foreign to us.
The land is ours.
Ours the sea and the sky,
the magic and the vision.
Companeros, here I see you dance
around the tree we are planting for communism.
Its prodigal wood resounds.

Priscilla Brown

THE COLOUR BLACK

I saw a portrait on a wall
emblem — so exquisite,
I saw a feather in a cap,
portraying a beautiful colour.
And I stared amazed at its colour.
The colour black, I said
The colour so beautiful, so bright.
The colour of so many beautiful things in life.

I walked along the dusty road,
and looked at my feet so distinguished on the ground.
The colour black, I said
The colour brown,
Why is it, I always see these beautiful colours
all around.

I listened to a voice so clear, so adequate, so
distinguished,
And I stared once more, even more than I'd once dare,
And then I whispered the Colour Black.

Oh, shut up, came a voice,
"Don't you see I'm brown like chocolate cream."
Another said, "I'm white like whipped cream."
How funny — I thought looking up,
And saw the colour black above.

Why, yes the colour Black,
Once unwanted, discriminated,
Ruled, Slaved and Humiliated.
But the colours that run in all our veins,
Are all the same.
Not cream nor white nor chocolate nor Black
So why confuse the colour BLACK.

Anielli J. Camrhal

POEM

Je crie ma peine
Je crie ma rage
A toi
A vous
Au monde
Je crache mon dégout
Je crache mon désespoir
Connais-tu ce mot mystérieux
Connaissez-vous ce mot magique
Le monde connait-il ce mot perdu
PAIX
J'élate ma colère

Je dérive dans mes larmes
Comme si l'Algérie
Ne suffisait pas
Comme si le Viet-Nam
Etait nécessaire
Et maintenant
Le Salvador...
Guerre
Guerre
Tonne, Eclate, Crépite
A quand la PAIX?
Que leur direz-vous?
Eux, Enfants du
Vingt et unième siecle
Que l'Algérie ne suffisait pas
Qu'il fallait le Viet-Nam
Et aussi le Salvador

Que leur direz-vous?

POEM

I scream out my pain
I scream out my rage
To you
and you there
and to the world
I spit out my disgust
I spit out my despair
Have you heard that mysterious word
You there have you heard that magic word
Has the world heard that misplaced word
PEACE
My fury bursts forth
I drift away in tears
As if Algeria
were not enough
As if Vietnam
were necessary
And now
El Salvador...
War
War
Exploding, Rattling, Thundering
When will we have PEACE?

You there — what will you tell them?
Those children of the
Twenty-first Century
That Algeria wasn't enough
That Vietnam and El Salvador too
were necessary

You there —
What will you tell them?

Rumeena

POEM

mi é bribi tak'
wan dé
wan pikin boi
wan pikin wentjé
sa opo en anoe
"Pa, dis' mi wan' gi joe
bika mi hati bigi
foe di joe na mi pa,
bika mi lobi joe"
lek' fa mi lobi joe
en mi hati bigi
foe di
wan dé
mi sa de
na mama
foe *oenoe* pikin

POEM

I believe that
someday
a little boy
a little girl
will open their hands
"Dad, I want to give you this
because I am big-hearted
because you are my dad,
because I love you"
just as I love you
and I am big-hearted
because
one day
I will be
the mother
of *our* children

Marie-Ella Williams

MASK

Pretty lady puts on her mask
Paints on her smile
glosses her frame in
shallow trappings.

Pretty lady your mask screens you
from what is real
The family you must nurture
the love you must give
the work you must do
It hides time
and protects you
for one instant
Then, like eye shadow
it blows away
leaving you bare.

Pretty lady
your mask covers specks
of discontent
festering inside your bosom
Pain
Anger
Weariness
Like a waxy buildup
it clings and mars.

Pretty lady
Clean off your mask!

Lillian Allen

IT'S NOT APATHY

(for Blanche)

I pause
To ease the load
Take a rest
A quiet inbreathe
Love a little
Nurture myself

Battered
All these years
Struggling
Struggling physically
Struggling mentally
Struggling emotionally

It's not apathy
I just want to ease the load
And take a rest
Close my eyes for a minute

Jennifer Rahim

SIGHT

Once I had pierced
the crystal surface
of rivers and marvelled
at the way my eyes could
peer through liquid walls
to behold subterranean
worlds

That was my prized power
until seasonal rains
brought down floods of
silt and soiled my sight
with mud

Now at the bottom of the
river time spins cycles
in secret and I must
wait until the mud
is washed away before
I can see behind the
walls.

Joy Mahabir

SUNDAY

Sunday we sit across the table
Comfortable, in comfortable lies.
Speaking with memories and gestures
Among pink ceramics and butterflies
Pressed in glass cases.
Forgetting too quickly
Our senses are linking,
Pretense comes too soon
To notice despair.
Ignoring the phrases
And laughter which terrorize
Long after, alone in dark sleep.

Niala Maharaj

INDIAN ARRIVAL DAY

Searching for my grandfather
For those bushy whiskers and that strange accent
Not mine, nor not India's either.
That thundering voice, And the rough blanket
The cocoa beans and ohrnis
I yearn for the girl's voice, pregnant with laughter
Reaching forward, offering
The smile in the eyes, sentences clouded with happiness.
And long to sit on the counter
And tell my stories.

Toni, tall and long-limbed
Put her arms around the shoulders of men.
And I cower into the memory of my grandfather
Who put his arms around me.

I did not love him.
His coffin was occasion for posturing.
Yet he is there
Like the ghost of the sarangee
When the vultures pick at my flesh.

And other men's thundering voices become tinny
Muffled in the draped folds of that long blanket
If only I could shake that blanket
Pull it away and say
"Why did you love me? Why did you love Me?"

But I ask it, instead, of my flesh
That leans toward my nephew
Veiling my eyes from his parents.

Mahadai Das

THE VAMP'S PRIZE

A brassy belt girded
her waist as impossibly
as her ringed and smoke-filled
intentions about the New Year Ball.

Her arms were costume-jewelled,
a rapier of gold along her elbow,
a sword of silver by her hip.
On her fingers were all the rings
of forgotten Cleopatras...

Her fifty-five-year breasts
in skintight blacks, sagged
under the strain to stand erect.

Jetblack curls were too perfect
a piece. Beneath her folding
chin, more jewels could be
hidden, or makeup end its
telltale mark in a comfortable crevice.

Her chin rose high
in a music-filled air.
A glittering purse
(with her secrets
of Methuselah) swung
with a measured swing
from her wrist.

Shiny earrings dangled
like last year's Christmas
decorations from her ear.

Community fathers
and the holy brotherhood
froze as she catwalked the length
of their fundraiser. Green
lucre laughed from her cleavage
as fullsuited fathers and tasteful
wives, obedient sons and girlfriends
turned their gaze away.

She didn't win, not a single
prize. A ragamuffin with a torn
denim at the knee, cheeks
ruddy as a rural filly,
carried the crown.

After, the women scorned "the vamp"
staring hard at the money
down her breasts, her
smoky kohl-drawn eyes.

Downing a gay whisky, she
ignored them. A long cigarette
theatrically held between her
ringed fingers, smoked
like a genie into night's promised air.

As I left an empty hall,
a last lavender balloon in my hand,
I saw that loser remove her shiny pumps,
then slowly, without prime prize or flesh
limp into New Year Morning.

Pauline Crawford

BITTER GLOOM

Death hangs over our heads
With bitter gloom
Death hangs over our heads
As cold and lonely as an empty tomb

Oppression! Depression! Starvation
A tek over di lan'
Babylon think of every evil plan
To add to the discomfort of man and woman
And if wi try fi change di situation

Death hangs over our heads
With bitter gloom
Death hangs over our heads
As cold and lonely as an empty tomb

Frustration! Confusion, Sufferation
A cause disunity 'mongst each an' everyone
All dem tings yah noh mus' lead to a revolution
Even if death hangs over our heads
With bitter gloom
As cold and lonely as an empty tomb

Desolation, Intimidation, Exploitation
The battle is for the strong
We must can find solutions
And do what we can
Or death will always hang
Over our heads
With bitter gloom
As cold and lonely as an empty tomb

Determination, Self-Examination, Organisation
Mek wi tek a firm stan'
An' mek some decision
Fi remove death from
Hanging over our heads with bitter gloom
Hanging over our heads
As cold and lonely as
An empty tomb

Honor Ford-Smith

AUX LEON...WOMEN

Before the sunlight
splits the dry rock
their eyes open
on coarse board walls and
guttered
government
land

mind set begins
with stumbling over
a sleeping child
an animal immobile

"catch up the fire/ scrape and grate the cassava/ carry the water
(uphill)/ boil the tea/ the toloma/ beat the castor oil seeds/
wash clothes/ nurse baby/ soothe old lady/ weed garden/ chop
banana/ load banana/ carry it down the stony road/
Un cadeau pour Monsieur Guise"
la lin coowee, coowee
la solei joo baway
(the moon runs
it runs
till the sun
catches it)
"how much are the bananas today/ the housewife said
unbuttoning her coat/ laying down her string bag in the
Islington shop/ hurry up there/ don't have all day/ she added
himself will be home soon and the tea not ready/ nothing
changes/ only the prices rise/ Gimme a dozen a them/ bruised
lot you got here today/"
la lin coowee, coowee
la solei joo baway
(the moon runs
it runs
till the sun
catches it)
scrape/ boil/ beat
"sleep baby sleep
father working far away
he give me something   i take it
he give me nothing   i take it"

Aux Leon women
This morning
when the sunlight strikes
the rock
Let us sweep that old yard clean.
Let us beat our quarrels into one voice
with the rhythm of the hardwood pestle.
Let us light our fires on this hillside
so all the islands will see
this labour is not free.
Let us burn the sweet wood
for its scent will fill the nostrils
of the blind and deaf.

listen
(la solei coowee coowee
la lin joo baway)
The stroke of a cutlass in water has no meaning
(la solei coowee coowee
la lin joo baway)
Listen, a song —
a song is beginning
right here
among us

(Note: Aux Leon is a small community in St. Lucia, situated near Dennery on the eastern side of the island and created by squatters on the high and rocky backlands of an old estate.)

Lorna Goodison

SHE WALKS INTO ROOMS

She walks into rooms
and they run for towels
say "girl, dry yourself."
And she says no, it's only light
playing upon my water-wave taffetta
dress
But her host put his hand to her face
and it came away wet.
Sometimes at nights
she has to change the sheets,
her favourite brown roses
on a lavender trellis
grow sodden
and that water has salt
in it
and that's no good for roses.
He left her all this water
to hold in the purple throat
of a flower
it overflowed onto the floors
and her silver shoes sailed
like moon-boats in it.
The water took all the curl
from her hair
It runs slick to her shoulders
where his hands spread
tributaries of rivers.
as he left he said
"It is time to learn to swim."
So saying, he departed to a dry place
carrying silver in his hair
and deep currents in his slightest
motion.
She could have died of cold waiting
in the wet he left there
But she grew full of mysteries
like the ocean.

A FORGIVENESS

Forgive yourself
for loving the Voodoo priest
who drinks your blood at night
through undermining tubes.
Forgive yourself for loving
the children of salt
who left their brine on you
so you dream always of waterfalls.
Take the base betrayals
stamped with deceit
throw them to the forgiving air
and invoke transmutation.
In time they will fall
as rains of redemption.
Forgive yourself for loving
sailors
with brass trunks
filled with lies
for loving flying stuntmen
when you needed earthbound
eyes.
Forgive yourself then
forgive yourself now
and know that you cannot change
someone
if only they would let you
love them
all changing (like yours)
is light from within
all you can be is witness,
and love yourself now
enough to know
that you are lit
and that light will draw
more light to itself
and that will be light
enough for a start
to new life and a self
forgiven heart
and being new
just be.

Ramabai Espinet

TAMANI: a cane-cutting woman

Dawn and the pitch awaken
To her blackening footsteps
Pawpaw stems
Send bubbles and flutes
Our mother knew the field
Where the BRONZED ONE walked
    The cane in crooked glee
    The cracked earth...

Her reassured limbs would not fall
Beneath his blue-eyed smile;
    Here a mongoose killed the snake
    Afterwards, a child, breaking canes
    Heard the horse and fled.
At twilight she stood alone
Her shining cutlass green with grass
The bison plodding low on the red land.

And now the story of presences
Lights the town..
In 'The Mission', shops are crowded
At home, the banked chulhah waits
Carat always keeps the fumes
Of cheap cane juice
— Rum, Rum and more Rum —
The door unlatched...

She remembers to hide the bullpistle,
His stumbling steps, the mule's slow canter,
Oh God, perhaps tonight
The black mule will not fall.

('The Mission' - a small town in Trinidad just outside of the
Malgretoute Estate, and now known as Princes Town)

Opal Palmer Adisa

MY LIFE

Mornings
I wash the matter
from my eyes
my mother roasts me
breadfruit to eat

My grandmother
hems my dress
that is my life
like who I vote for
and what I call myself

In my country
night
is a black coal
and day a
sun-flower
we understand
things without
having to classify them

Grandpa
doesn't understand
how sharing his yams
with his friend, Brother Joseph,
is communistic

Father says he has nothing
against "ISM's" capital or otherwise
but he tastes gall
when he sees people
living in card-board shacks
and digging through garbage bins
for food
and that is
an example of democracy

Where we live
is called
primitive, undeveloped
we are certain the naming
is significant
as our rules
are few and simple
we don't
harbor
liars
thieves
or murderers
they are as
hunger,
homelessness
and needing an ID
to be out
South Africa and
U.S.A. are synonymous

Claire Harris

OF IRON, BARS AND CAGES

in	late summer evening softens angularities	*in*
half light	emphasises the roundness of women and hills	*the rented*
pliers	we four stare through drought dried grass	*room*
approach	to where below us the river deepens into black	*under*
the hair	above the brick-red massive rise of the	*half light*
the grey	General bears down on small dreams we swirl	*she*
hair	ice in our half finished drinks and sigh	*crazed*
the soft	women we sit as at the bottom of wells	*by the hours*
female hair	darkness and smooth sides crouched in cold	*of children*
that curls	we have only the strands of thin years	*trapped*
steel	to weave ladders strong enough to lift us to	*in the empty*
snaps	the round circles of sky yet like spiders	*pocket*
pliers	grown accustomed to dark we take a sensuous	*in charity*
tug	pleasure in the intricate manouevres of our	*drained*
naked	weaving we talk of strategies discuss	*of hope*
the mount	technique and image then note the passing	*calls out*
of her	glory of the year and steep ourselves in	*for an adult*
who asked	sadness what we would like is a rope	*body*
for a name	let down from the blue heavens from	*a male body*
who needed	that dark cloud shaped like a hand a sign	*any body*
only the name	on which we could climb could ride	*to ride her*
of a death	to an immense and furious life	*furious heart*

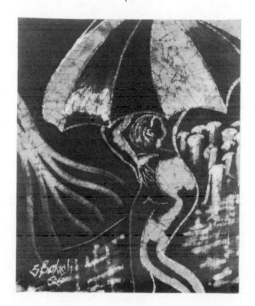

The Praise Singer

Christine Craig

ISLAND

In St. Kitts a child paused,
turned back to smile full
into my eyes, her face
a dark flower with sun
on her lashes. For that moment
my face in the shade, yours
in the sun, my years, your youth
recognition trembles between us.

You pause, just ready to grow up.
Your smile says — I will be a woman
like you, my smile says, you are
pure delight. In that flash
of love and homage we know
it is sweet to be female.

In the curve of the beach
in the swell of the hills
in the flush of orchids
in the tangled rain forests
in the sweet order of farmlands
see across these islands
our daughters are growing
all our beauty
all our riches
are one.

R.H. Douglas

IN CELEBRATION...

In Celebration of Womanhood...
Celebrate Womanhood!
Come on, all you sisters,
Celebrate!
Celebrate Womanhood!
Forget the shackles and
chains of past painful
relationships.
Celebrate your relationship
with self.....
Yourself.

In Womanhood
we stride...
One *sure* step at
a time.

No hesitation
No limitation
No back sliding
Onward...
Forward...sisters...March
with all your confidence
into Womanhood.

Celebrate!
Yes, celebrate Womanhood!
For to achieve Womanhood
takes guts and belly
and brain
Seldom beauty...
for Beauty is a thing
that seems to keep you
forever in search of
admiration...
not in search of
introspection.

Look, sisters!
Look within,
and celebrate, Womanhood!

Louise Bennett

BANS O' OOMAN!

On the launching of the Jamaica Federation of Women for
women of all classes *"high and low, miggle, suspended"*...

Bans o' ooman! Bans o' ooman!
Pack de place from top to grung
Massa lawd, me never know sey
So much ooman deh a Tung!

Up de step and dung de passage
Up de isle an dung de wall
Not a Sunday-evening Hope tram
Pack like St. George Hall.

De ooman dem tun out fe hear
How Federation gwan.
Me never se such diffrent grade an
Kine o' ooman from me bawn.

Full dress, half dress, tidy — so-so
From bare y'eye to square-cut glass,
High an low, miggle, suspended,
Every diffrent kine o' class.

Some time dem tan so quiet, yuh
Could hear a eye-lash drop,
An wen sinting overseet dem,
Lawd, yuh want hear ooman clap —

Me was a-dead fe go inside
But wen me start fe try,
Ooman queeze me, ooman push me,
Ooman frown an cut dem y'eye.

Me tek me time an crawl out back
Me noh meck no alarm,
But me practice bans o' tactics
Till me ketch up a platform.

Is dat time me se de ooman dem
Like variegated ants,
Dem face a-bus wid joy fe sey,
"At las' we got we chance".

Ef yuh ever hear dem program!
Ef yuh ever hear dem plan!
Ef yuh ever hear de sinting
Ooman gwine go do to man!
Federation boun to flourish,
For dem got bans o' nice plan.
An now dem got de heart an soul
Of true Jamaica ooman

Deborah Singh-Ramlochan

ONE TRIBE

of the tribe
woman
pale skinned
long haired
or cropped short
darkly gleaming
ebony
copper tones
Beautiful
frail
strong
Woman
searching
questing
seeking forever
questions.
To which most find
there are no simple answers
Our emotions cut deep
Our hurt runs in rivers
Our love soars
Life...creases us with age
wrinkled memories
are sustained
in alert
twinkling eyes.
Never to be quenched
It is a heady
high feeling
just being
this woman
one unit
of the vast
tribe

Meryl James-Bryan

IN THANKSGIVING

Ah want to take off meh hat to women...Caribbean women.
Burnished ebony and copper skins; and firm solid flesh; and
strong white teeth tipped with gold.
Arms as strong and graceful as coconut trees, with a thousand
jingles...
gold and silver bracelets, musically accompanying every move.
Floppy Panama hats, gay head ties and regal airs
Firm breasts that suckled a thousand brown babies, and saucy
rounded buttocks that rock and roll as if struggling against con-
tainment.
Africa. Proud, bold and determined, in spite of Europe.

Ah want to pay tribute to Caribbean women.
To those who were, and are, and might have been.
To those who will be, despite the evils from afar
That try in vain to control our destiny
To those who broke through the lady chains; and the colour
chains;
and the picki-hair chains; and the thick-lip chains; and the flat-
nose chains;
and the middle-class chains; and the gossip chains; and the
Europe chains.
To those who suffered silently their wandering men
And those who cunningly dropped an idea, then quietly let
their men take the credit
Eve was not all evil; Nefertiti, a real beauty.

Ah want to say thanks to Caribbean women.
To Lila St. Hill..and Sybil James...and Glen Byam...and Audrey
Jeffers...and Elaine Thorne...and Dada...and Beryl Mc-
Burnie...and Molly Ahye...and Calypso Rose...and Louise Ben-
nett...and Mrs. P...and Miss Delcina...and Auntie Kay...and
Amy Garvey...and Beverly Jones...and Tourist Annie too.
Yes ah want to thank them all
For giving me the strength and courage to deal.
For carving a helluva path to follow
May Sojourner Truth continue to reign in us all!

HONEY AND LIME

Yo soy mujer. Caribbean Woman.
With the grace of the Limbo dancer
the sexuality of the Wabine
and the persistence of the Deputy.

Je suis femme. Caribbean Woman.
With the strength of the Flag-woman
the independence of the Market-woman
and the brazenness of the Jamette.

I am woman. Caribbean Woman.
Powerful as the Orisa Mother
Fervent as the Baptist Preacher
Creative as the Calypsonian
Committed as the Pannist
Patient as the Housewife
and own-way as the Fisher-woman.

Erect as the Water-carrier
Dainty as the Hibiscus
Proud as the coconut trees
Fiery as the noon-day sun
Storm as a hurricane
But gentle as Oya's breath

I am woman. Caribbean Woman.
Complex, and with my share of contradictions
and a full dose of bitter-sweetness
But with an African resilience
Purely and surely-Caribbean Woman
in her all-encompassing entirety.

Christene Clarkson

WOMAN

Thy name is 'Woman'
Thy name is 'Mother'
You alone can "feel" first life
You alone know the touch of the unborn

You are creation's flowers
For from you comes the male
And from him comes the seed of life
A seed with little power
until it manifests itself
Growing deep within you —
The Woman, the Mother

You alone can nurture the seed of man
And feel it grow and grow
Till your belly bulges —
with the love of creation
Fiery form of love
Look upon thyself!
You resemble your brother man
But you are different...
Where else did nature merge —
strength and tenderness so completely
Than in you the woman, the mother

You are like a soft petal
Kissed by the tropical sun in early morning
Yet, you are Vibrant
    Determined
    And strong...
Woman, you are forever.

Nydia Ecury

HABAI

Machi bieu,
ta resa bo ta resa
òf t'un bon konseho
bo ta sigui ripití,
ku bo boka slap
kontinuamente
ta kou sin djente
den un ritmo di bo so?

Machi leu, hei!
Ta strika bo ta strika
dril ku kaki ku kashimir
òf ta un karisia
di den pasado
bo ke rebibá
ku bo mannan korkobá
den konstante moveshon?

Machi kèns,
ta friu bo tin
den tempu di kalor
òf ta miedu di etèrnidat
to pone bo garganta
tur na lòpchi
tambaliá
pa indiká ku
nò,
aindo nò?

Machi prenda,
ku bo benanan di kalki,
bo lomba di baul,
bo wowonan nublá,
mi ke bo pa mi bebi:
zoyoba — yayabo — stimabo
maske ta ún anochi
promé bo bira inmóbil,
promé bo bira kos,
ketu...
friu...

OLD LADY

Lil' old lady,
are you saying prayers
or do you keep repeating
some sound advice,
that your shapeless mouth
chews constantly
in a rhythm
all your own?

Silly old lady,
are you ironing
your family's laundry once again
or do you wish
to bring to life
a caress of years gone by,
that your gnarled hands
are so busily occupied?

Daft old lady,
do you feel cold
in summer heat
or does your sinewy neck
upon a call from eternity
shake to indicate
your need
to stay with us,
yet another little while?

Sweet old lady,
with your clogged up veins,
your widow's hump.
your eyes opaque,
I'll have you for my baby,
for a single night, at least,
to hug you — kiss you — love you
before you cease the movements,
before you turn into an object,
cold and still...

Marina Ama Omowale Maxwell

TO MY GRANDMOTHER, LADY-WOMAN

I wasn't there
when you died
when they laid you out
               as you had lived, a little starchy
stiffly
from your middle parted hair, old bun
resting
to your bunioned feet.

I wasn't there
when they stopped you,
               as you had lived, ever moving on

Walking, walking, ever walking
to feed poor children
giving them their break/
fast
shed
with your coterie of tears.

But I remember
a firm dignity of wrinkles
brown-lined face
and thinking, thinking, ever thinking eyes.

I remember
your endless scholarships for poor girls
and boys
giving them their break/
fast
with your black leather encased bunioned feet
worn shoes, walking
shaped to the bunions of your pain.

It is your brown song you poured into my mother's face
your strength
that kept her back straight up
as she too
Red Crossed the white world, our melee world
Head high
Her tiny feet treading paths unknown
for women
then.

It is your bundled self
with your great sloping shoulders
that you gave to her
and passed
into my song.

IF I CARRY BANNERS
THEN AND NOW
IT IS YOUR SONG
AND HERS
THAT I SALUTE

Cornelia Frettlöh

JUST LIKE WATER

I am a woman, just like water, soft, tender and fragile.

My mother is a spring, high up in the evergreen mountains, a
never exhaused source of an inaccessible ebony secret. Begot-
ten in an explosion, an outburst of wild desire and love. My
Father, the volcano, spitted his burning how torrents into the
sky. Wasn't I born in heaven, a goddess of dawn?
I am a girl, young lady and mother, a whore, lover and friend.
I am a witch, divinity's sister, a slave of myself and man.

But I am a woman, just like water, generating current, running
machines.

A sweet tiny river, I suddenly tumble, rising my weakness to powerful strength. Jubilating cascades, dark roaring falls; disguised in my white cloudy steam dress I charm away all edges and jags. I put a spell on proud noble rocks, lead them astray, leaving behind me smooth polished stones.

But I am a woman, just like water, quiet and silent, patient and still.

Am I not the lake whose shining surface reflects your self?
An invisible marble thrown into me will always send signals.
Ring after ring, eternal and deep.
But I am a woman, just like water, fed with hopes and meanwhile dried up.

The might and glory of a sun absorbed me, el sol, le soleil.
Dreams and promises evaporated to infinity, a nothingness with wings.

But listen, el sol and le soleil, I am a woman, just like water, and I will be back again.

I will be the rain, reborn in the deepest ocean, leaving the salt of my tears behind. I will be the constant drizzle, heavy shower and flooding storm.

I am a woman, just like water, sweet, soft and strong, the rain of the rainbow.

Lorraine F. Joseph

BLACK GIRL IN THE RAIN

Hey little girl
with your
high crowned
natural head
thrown back to laugh
as the rain runs down your face.

Cares forgot
Hair forgot
Drawn up in
tight little curls
that grace your sunbaked brow.

Spin,
    Dance,
            Enjoy the rain's warm fingers,
                tickling, teasing ecstasy.

Lydia Geerman

POEM B

Tur generasho di nobo
mester eksperensha
siklonan di bida
ku tur tempo a konta.
Ripiti erornan ya kometí
eksperimentá ekibokashonnan bon konosí
keda pegá den trampanan skondí
di tiniebla di un solo atardi.
Gosa dushi di amor
siña guli marga di su sabor.
Konosé furia, duele i pordon
tochi nubia ku bo man.
Parti dje rutina di bida
ser humiyá mas ku elogiá.
Enfermedat o aksidente
ta pone nos pendiente
dje destino di nos tur.

Est'un sueltu mundo tin
ku ainda tin muhé
yen di zjeitu pa bibé
traha bida i kuidé,
ya historia por ripiti su mes
den sirkulonan será, no tur ora mes bon planifiká!

POEM B

All generations once again
must experience
cycles of life
which all times served.
Repeat errors already made
experiment with well known mistakes
get caught in hidden traps
in the dusk of a single afternoon
savour the sweetness of love
learn to swallow her bitter taste.
Get acquainted with rage, sorrow and pardon
touch the sky with one's hands.

Part of life's routine
receives humiliation more than recognition.
Illness or accident
can make us uncertain
of the destiny
we all have to face.

What a piece of luck
our world still has women
full of swing to live,
give birth and take care of life,
so history can repeat itself
in closed circles,
not always as well planned as we'd like it to be.

Pauline Crawford

AN AFRICAN CHILD IS BORN

Life began
in the womb of an African woman
life continued
with food from mother nature
and the growth that each new
        day brings
she makes her appearance into the world
        into the world
an African child is born
as delicate as the petals
        of a rose
fresh as the morning dew
God's gift, God's wonderful gift
welcome to the world.

Each new day she grows
until she buds and blossoms
into a beautiful African woman
with tilted chin and poise
as graceful as a swan
each move perfectly timed
standing tall, sturdy and strong
God's gift, God's special gift

Take your place in the world

Young vibrant and swift as
a young fox
skin dark and smooth as
    starapple skin
and smells like apple
    blossoms in the early morning
majestic as a full moon in a
    cloudless sky
beautiful as an evening
    sunset across the sea
special as the morning sunrise
she is firmly planted
she is deep rooted
unshakable she stands
long will she live on this earth
she is God's gift
God's perfect gift
challenge the world!

Gladys August Hall

TRIBUTE TO A WOMAN

And she was born —
    and watched —
            and grew up to be a lady.
Her life patterned for her by society.

"No change," she said.
    "A housewife
            a mother
                    a domestic
Or just the lowly thought
    of a nurse
            a midwife
                    a stenographer
                            a teacher

Perhaps a clerk
　　a telephone operator
Or even a newscaster.

But never a banker
　　a doctor
　　　　an aviator
　　　　　　or an astronaut

Maybe yes
　　a senator
　　　　a mayor
　　　　　　a vice somebody

Perhaps
　　a prime minister
　　　　a president."
And these open injustices keep haunting
　　her mind
　　　　her soul
　　　　　　her very being

As she watches the pattern,
　　and everything
　　　　becomes rote
Her mate
　　her government
　　　　her job
　　　　　　her very way of life,
Her destiny all worked out for her.
And she is ridiculed
　　　　dissatisfied
　　　　　　limited
　　　　　　　　tormented.

And her inner 'self' surges forth,
　　And she is born anew.
And her 'self' takes over —
　　　　　　her ability
　　　　　　　　and knowledge
　　　　　　　　　　and power
　　　　　　　　　　　　and respect
　　　　　　　　　　　　　　and ambition

And she becomes
              demanding
                 upgrading
                      EQUAL

AND A WOMAN

And now:
              She dares to choose her way of life
              To expose her dignity, And show
              That she too can play her part
                    and contribute
                          in the business world
                                and sciences

And SHE is recognised.

Nelcia Robinson

YOUNG WOMAN

Young Woman, fragile shoot
I am afraid for you
You are so vulnerable.

Young Woman, Tender vine
I am afraid for you
You are denied guidance,

Young Woman, slender leafy plant
I am afraid for you
You are so innocent
Glorying the discovery
Of your beauty.

Young Woman, blossoming palm-tree
You are on the threshold
Of life in all its fullness
I am afraid for you
You are exposed to the elements
Of violence, disillusionment
and discrimination,
Fruits of an unjust social and
economic arrangement.
Young Woman
Be a sealed fountain
In an enclosed garden
Whose walls are to be scaled
When you are Woman, Conscious, Positive,
Goal setting, Confident Woman.

Young Woman, be wise
Guard you dignity
Acknowledge your potential.

Father, Mother, Older Man, Older Woman,
Uncle, Aunt, Brother, Sister, Young Woman,
Be a hedge around her
Bruise not the flower.

Vanda Radzik

LINGUISTICS #1: BREAKDOWN

Woman,
And the tongue twists over woe
or womb
(man speaks glibly enough for itself)
Naturally,
The stress is on the first —
Strange muted syllable though it seem,
Its utterance does require some effort
I can guarantee.
Rather like the uncanny blow of the conch shell
full bodied, irrefutable,
with all the world of the untold sea within.

This is the tone that matters
Not the imposed limitation of one tongue, one type
Or the varied play on some word-filled idea.
I demur,
It is not enough to be but partly whole:
Wohin woman?
From each we strain our soul.

Judith Behrendt

"NASARAYABA"

I am an old woman now.
I carry dead dry wood,
On my greying head,
As I walk in the cool morning dew
From farm.
Wood for the fire
Wood to burn
Heavy dead weight,
Like my bones.

When I was young, I walked
Like the young girls, proudly.
The bundle then
Was a baby nestled
In my plump arms.
A bright black-eyed pickney
Tiny mouth sucking at my breast.
Drinking greedily from
My (then) green bones.
Oh, to be young again,
To feel that live weight (so light)
Lifting me into my life
Rather than this heavy
Dead load on my head
That pounds me
Like a hammer
Down into my grave.

But the load
Will be burned

And its heat
Will melt the ice in me.
And I'll rise again
(As I did in my short, hard life)
Triumphant, out of ashes.

("Nasarayaba" means "I rise again" in Garifuna or Black Carib, the
language of the narrator)

Shirley Small

WOMEN OF BULAWAYO AND OTHERS

The world salutes
those women who grasp weapons
to defend their dignity;
who — tagged, curfewed, barbed-wired —
vent their fury and hurl their demands
with sticks and stones
at murderous Goliaths;
women, heart-burdened with distress,
for horror is their life-time mate.

The world waits silently to hear
the protests silent sisters
hurl against oppressors
who sacrifice their progeny
as patriotic gun-fodder
— sacrifice that inflicts
equally impotent sisters
with parallel sacrifice.

Gladys Waterberg

SERY

You are the root
the mother of our struggle
in your footsteps
we are marching forward
shall never turn back

SERY

Mother of our struggle
our righteous struggle
brought us all together
one day
to remember
your words
don't tell lies.........
brace yourself
for victory day

MEKI WI SORI WI EYGI KRAKTI

Sisa mek' wi opo luku now
wan fasi fa sranan kan bow
Sisa mek' wi opo lusu wi skin
bika wi ooktu na doti pikin
Tumsi langa wi de wakti
kon mek' wi sori wi eygi krakti

No tenapu more na seysey
ma mek' wi dyompo me a strey
Fu prani wroko nanga leri-man
di e suku wan fasi fu bow sranan
Tumsi langa wi e wakti
kon meki wi sori wi eygi krakti

Sisa fo hondro tenti yari
wi ben suku wan okasi
fu man seti wi eygi tori
a ten doro mek' ei grabu hori
tumsi langa wi e wakti
kon mek' wi sori wi eygi krakti

Opo yu sten, yu no afu fu frede
wi sa strey gi na leti ede na ede
no mek' no wan man kon kori yu
bika wortu lay ma na du mus'du
Tumsi langa wi e wakti
kon mek'we sori wi eygi krakti

LET US SHOW OUR OWN STRENGTH

Sisters stand up and look around now
Search a way to build Suriname
Sisters stand up and shake you body
because we also are children from the land

Too long we have been waiting
come let us show our own strength

Don't stand at the side-lines any longer
but let us jump into the struggle
to sow workers and intellectuals
who are searching a way to build Suriname

Too long we have been waiting
come let us show our own strength

Sisters for hundreds of years already
we have been searching for the chance
to settle our own matters
the time is ripe let us hold on

Too long we have been waiting
come let us show our own strength

raise your voice have no fear
we shall struggle
for the rights
side by side

Tiffany Robinson

THE LIONESS

Roaring and growling
she makes claim
On
all the bodies

Ferocious, she comes
striding,
defying,
inveigling.

Hungry for food,
another kind
She stealthily
hunts.

Suspicious
capricious
not famished
but ....

This lioness
has
a lot of
concupiscence.

Celene Jack

WOMAN OF SOUTH AFRICA

You who watch
Your children
Die of hunger
Because there is no food to eat.

You who watch
Your children gripped by fear
And lack of hope
As they see no way out.

You who watch your children
seized and murdered
When they dare to rise up
Against the Oppressors.
You who watch
Your children
Detained by security
For months and months
Without a trial

You who watch your rights denied
To see your husband as you wish

You who watch
With tears of anger
Your human rights exterminated
In the new Repressive Laws.
You who watch
With courage
But are refused a reason
For all this suffering.

I salute You
Woman of South Africa!

Ahdri Zhina Mandiela

SPESHAL RIKWES

speshal rikwes
to dih ilan possie
for babbilan still ah try ole I
awndah slavery

ah membah wen
chain shackle I foot
now ah men-made leddah wintah boot
an in times before
men in a klan
cum wid dem plan
fih mash dung I state
as man an ooman
but I naw guh back
an dwell pan pass attacks
instead I ah mek a fahwud check
wid dis
speshal rikwes

speshal rikwes
from a yearnin ungah
burnin burnin
burnin in dih mind of
of a city-bred yout
speshal rikwes fih dih trute

speshal rikwes
fih dih bones in dih sands
of dih Carrybeyan lands
fih wih urtin spirits debri
speshal rikwes fih you
an fih me

fih dih skills
of dih uprooted ones
widout birtlan
wukkin fih fahrin investment plans
inna Merrrica, Sout Afrikka
Cannada an Inglan
inna dis yah babbilan

speshal rikwes fih I lan

fih dih blud ah dih eart
dih sawff red dirt
dat we fawt to preserve
fih wih own pots of clay
while dem watch evvy day
an say: MEK DEM PAY! MEK DEM PAY!
suh ow now I mus res
from makin dis
speshal rikwes?

wen dem ah try dem bes
fih keep I awndah stress
an covah dung I success
wid dem IQ tes
usin dem bans an bans
ah propaganda wagons
from dih still-bawn creashan
of dem feeble ans

but yuh know
sumting gawn wrong
wid dem plan
for look: I still ah stan strong
an I ah call to all ones
(fih elp clean up dih mess)
wid dis
speshal rikwes

speshal rikwes
espeshally
fih dih natives
sedated an apathy-stated
by apawtide: all roun dih worl

for apawt from I
dem hide/dem hide
an seek fih mek I weak

but since JAH bless I
wid strent
fih strive an relent
I wih stan up an projek
forevah: dis speshal rikwes

speshal rikwes fih dih ilan possie
speshal rikwes fih you an fih me

Biographies

OPAL PALMER ADISA (Jamaica/U.S.A.)

1954- She is "first and foremost a writer," in addition to being a teacher, storyteller, director and community organizer. She says that her work is shaped by her roots. Her publications include *Pina, The Many-Eyed Fruit* (1985), and *Bake-Face and Other Guava Stories* (1986).

LILLIAN ALLEN (Jamaica/Canada)

She is a writer who is best known for Dub poetry. She has won two Juno awards for poetry with music. She lives in Toronto where she works as a consultant on culture, creativity and community development. She also writes short fiction and children's poetry and stories.

PHYLLIS SHAND ALLFREY (The Commonwealth of Dominica)

1908-1986. She was a writer, a socialist thinker, an activist and a politician. When the Federation of the West Indies came into being, she served as its only female minister until its collapse (1958-1962). She founded *The Star* and was its editor and chief writer until it folded in 1982. Her publications include *The Orchid House* (1953), *In Circles* (1940) and *Palm and Oak* (1950).

KARIN AMMON (Trinidad and Tobago)

1962- She is a child clinical psychologist who loves writing and has always written essays and poetry. She is conducting research in the area of childbirth, experimenting with different methods in order to lessen the pain involved.

LYNETTE ATWELL (Trinidad and Tobago)

1938- She works in the field of town and country planning. She has been writing poetry since she was ten, and seriously since 1977. Her special interest is in Caribbean cookery — she has written numerous articles and is working on a cookbook. She has published poetry and articles in the *Trinidad and Tobago Review*.

343

JUDITH BEHRENDT (Belize)

1947- She works in family planning "to help women control their fertility, essential to equality." She says that she was "born a feminist, poet, writer, dreamer." She started writing at age 16 and has been greatly influenced by the work of Anais Nin. She has published short stories and poems in *The Feminist Voice*.

LOUISE BENNETT (Jamaica/Canada)

She has been described as Jamaica's leading comedienne, as the "only poet who has really hit the truth about her society through it own language." A British Council Scholarship took her to the Royal Academy of Dramatic Art where she studied in the late forties. She had her own B.B.C. program (World Service) called Caribbean Carnival. She has received many awards in recognition for her outstanding contribution to Jamaican cultural life: Doctorate of Literature from the University of the West Indies, the Order of Jamaica and the Manley Award for Excellence.

KAMLA BEST (Trinidad and Tobago/France)

She is a writer of poetry. Her poems have been published in the *Trinidad and Tobago Review*.

SANDRA BIHARI (Suriname)

1971- She is a student. Her special love is reading, especially about the youth and women in other Caribbean countries. "People find me a difficult person when I talk about subjects like the homeless people they don't care about. That's why I write poems."

JEAN BINTA BREEZE (Jamaica/U.K.)

She is a mother and dub poet. She was a teacher of English and Drama in her home parish of Hanover. She was also a cultural organizer with the Jamaican Cultural Commission and trained at Jamaica's School of Drama. With Mutabaruka she produced her first recording "Slip yuh fool' yu neva go to an African school." She has appeared in Reggae Sun Splash and has published a book of poems, *Answers*.

PRISCILLA BROWN (Belize)
1965- She is a primary school teacher. "I write a great deal of songs and poems most of which are kept in my personal file. My greatest desires are to become a pharmacist and to sing before a great audience someday!!"

ROSANNE BRUNTON (Trinidad and Tobago)
1951- She is a graduate student in Comparative Literature. Her areas of interest are women in Third World Literature and Third World Literature in general. She has been active in the women's movement in Trinidad and Tobago. Her publications include academic essays and a short story, "Rum Sweet Rum," published in the *Trinidad and Tobago Review*, 1984.

A. M. BURGOS (Suriname)
1952- She is a biologist/entomologist. She started writing poetry while very young. "Being afraid of having written something silly and perhaps afraid of showing my feelings, I used to tear up my poems shortly after I had written them....The publications of these poems by CAFRA is a stimulus to continue writing."

ANIELLI J. CAMRHAL (Martinique)
1953- She is a French and English teacher. She writes of herself, "J'ai toujours été fascinée par les MOTS. Pourtant, pendant longtemps j'ai refusé toutes formes d'écriture. Et puis, un jour les MOTS m'ont envahie et depuis je les ai acceptés."
"I have always been fascinated by WORDS. However for a long time, I refused all kinds of creative writing. And then, one day WORDS invaded me and since that moment, I have accepted them."

PEGGY CARR (St. Vincent and the Grenadines)
She is a journalist and poet who has been writing for many years. She won second prize in the BBC's Caribbean poetry competition. Her first published collection is called *Echoes from a Lonely Nightwatch*.

CHRISTENE CLARKSON (Grenada)
1954- She is a teacher of Biology and Spanish. She is also a member of the National Folk Theatre of Grenada and represented her country at CARIFESTA 1981 in Barbados and at FESTAG in Guadeloupe in 1986 as a dramatist/singer/poet. She has directed and played leading roles in several plays.

MICHELLE CLIFF (Jamaica/U.S.A.)
1946- She is a writer and teacher. "I was transported to America when I was three and spent my early life in the milieu of Jamaicans in New York. I was educated in Jamaica, America and England. My work is a search into the diasporic experience, the multi-ethnic identity, trying to forge wholeness from what appears to be fragmented." Her publications include *No Telephone to Heaven* (1987), *The Land of Look Behind* (1985), and *Abeng* (1984).

MERLE COLLINS (Grenada/U.K.)
She was raised in Grenada and worked there as a teacher and researcher. She was a member of the Grenada National Women's Organization until 1983. An accomplished poet, her work has appeared in a number of anthologies and in her own collection *Because the Dawn Breaks*, Karia Press 1985. She co-edited an anthology, *Watchers and Seekers*, Women's Press, London, 1987. She lives in England.

AFUA COOPER (Jamaica/Canada)
She was born in Jamaica and has lived in Toronto, Canada, since 1980. She is known as one of Toronto's talented young poets and has to date published two books of poetry: *Breaking Chains (1983) and Red Caterpillar on College Street* (1989). She is currently working on two manuscripts of poetry. A graduate student, Afua is completing her Master's degree in history at the Ontario Institute for Studies in Education, University of Toronto. Already knowing that poetry is her destiny, she also hopes to be an Africanist historian. Central to her life is her son Akil who is most wonderful.

MADELINE COOPSAMMY (Trinidad and Tobago/Canada)
She teaches English to immigrant children in Winnipeg. She studied in India and in Canada. Her Master's thesis was in the area of Multicultural Education in the Canadian School System. Her poetry has been published in *A Shapely Fire: Changing Literary Landscape*, and in *Other Voices: Writings by Blacks in Canada*.

CHRISTINE CRAIG *(Jamaica)*

She is a writer who lives with her two daughters in Kingston, Jamaica. Her first published works were the texts for two full-colour children's books produced by her husband, Karl Craig, and published by Oxford University Press in 1970. She has produced several non-fiction publications and training manuals on feminist and health topics. Her short stories and poems have been published in local, British and American anthologies and journals. Her first collection of poems, *Quadrille for Tigers was published in 1984 by Mina Press, Berkeley, California.*

PAULINE CRAWFORD *(Jamaica)*

1957- She is a teacher and actress. She writes of herself, "I have been working full-time with a group of working-class women called the Sistren Theatre Collective on issues affecting women for the past eleven years."

CHEZA DAILEY *(U.S. Virgin Islands)*

1957- She is an artist/teacher/poet/singer. She was "born and raised in New York City, where I truly never felt at home. It has been my interest to combine theatre/arts with education as a learning vehicle. I returned to my mother's home land, St. Croix, 5 1/2 years ago. I have found my mother's birth place to be an invigorating source of growth and development..."

NYDIA BRUCE DANIEL *(Trinidad and Tobago)*

1917- She was a primary school teacher and training supervisor in telephony, and is now retired. Her hobbies are sewing and writing poetry. Her poetry has been published in Trinidad and Tobago in the local newspapers and in *The School Paper* by the Ministry of Education

MAHADAI DAS *(Guyana)*

She was born in Guyana which she left in the 1980s. She was studying Philosophy at the University of Chicago when she became severely ill. She has since returned to Guyana where she continues to write. Her publications include: *I Want to be a Poetess of my People, My Finer Steel Will Grow* and *Bones.*

MARIA C. DIWAN (Curaçao)

1939- She works as a secretary. She has written numerous children's stories, produces Christmas cards, and has adapted an old card game for children in Papiamento — BONKUNECHI. Her stories have been included in the publications *Dakue Di Kuenta*, and *Chimichimi*.

GLADYS DO REGO-KUSTER (Curaçao)

1948- She is a social and cultural worker and served as President of the women's organization Union di Muhe Antiano (UMA) between 1975-1986. She has written several scripts for documentary films about women. At present she is involved in a wide-ranging project on women and sex-education. Her poems have been published in *Tribunal* (1973), *Bosero* (1977-84), and in *Chimichimi* (1981), among others.

R. H. DOUGLAS (Trinidad and Tobago)

1949- She is a writer and works as creative director of an advertising agency. She is also a member of the group "Media for Women" and vice-president of the Writers' Union of Trinidad and Tobago. Her poetry has been published in *New Voices, Trinidad and Tobago Review*, and *The Writer's Magazine*.

NYDIA ECURY (Curaçao)

She was born in Aruba, and has lived in Curaçao since 1957. She has been active in theatre, since 1959, as a translator, director and actress. Her publications include *Tres Rosea* (with two other poets), *Bos di Sanger and Na mi Kurasou Mara*. She has also written and published children's stories.

USHANDA IO ELIMA (U.S.A./Belize)

She is a teacher of Psychology and English as a second language. She has been a resident of Belize for the last 3 years. She is actively concerned about issues affecting women and children.

ZOILA M. ELLIS (Belize)

1957- She is an attorney by profession and is also involved in women's affairs. She has served as president of the Belize Organization for Women and Development (BOWAND). She states that "I have been writing poetry sporadically since I was 8 years old."

AIMÉE ELOIDIN *(Martinique)*

1958- She is a teacher of English and writes of herself, "J'ai commencé a ressentir la nécessité d'écrire à l'age de 14 ans. Mes premiers poèmes et mes premières nouvelles sont alors nés: C'était en 1971. Pendant quatre ans, je n'ai plus rien ecrit. Un jour, un ami tres cher m'a dit: "Quand tu as de la peine, ecris! Exorcise ton chagrin en le couchant sur le papier. Ecris et tu verras, tu ne seras plus triste! Il avait surement raison car je me sens mieux maintenant. L'écriture est ma thérapeutique."

RAMABAI ESPINET *(Trinidad and Tobago/Canada)*

1948- She is a writer and a researcher in literature and women's studies. "Writing is all I ever wanted to do; how to do it was the great mystery." She has been active in the women's movement in the Caribbean and in Canada. Her publications include essays and her poetry has been published in *CAFRA News, Trinidad and Tobago Review, Woman Speak, Fireweed, Toronto South Asian Review* and *Jahaji Bhai.*

EVELYNE *(Guyana/Canada)*

1915- She occupies herself with "learning, doing and zestful living." She writes of herself, "A feminist from the early 50's, I have had varied roles and experiences which have given me a patina shown in my enjoyment of life." Her work has been published in *Sandesto, The Sunday Graphic, The Mirror, Inter Caribbean, Indian Frontiers Magazine,* and *Indo-Caribbean Review.*

LIMA FABIEN *(Martinique)*

1964- She is an actress and writes of herself, "Passionnee de poesie. Ecrivant depuis l'age de 17 ans periode pendant laquelle elle eut son premier contact avec la poesie que devint par la suite une passion. Ses themes: c'est la contact avec la nature et toutes les petites choses de la vie melees a un cote sentimental qui est pour elle une source d'inspiration." She has published "Un Point de Vue" in *Pensee Universelle* (1983).

HONOR FORD-SMITH *(Jamaica)*

1951- She is an actress, a playwright and a writer, and is the founding Artistic Director of the Sistren Theatre Collective of Jamaica, for whom she has written and directed many plays. She has worked with Sistren towards developing a methodology of collective creation and has also been active in the women's movement in the Caribbean. She is the editor and co-author of *Lionheart Gal: Life Stories of Jamaican Women* and has written numerous articles on popular theatre, women's history in Jamaica and the theory and practice of Sistren.

BERNICE FRASER (Guyana/U.S.A.)
She is an educator in the teaching of English and lectured for several years at the University of Guyana in the Teacher Education Program. She writes of herself, "At the present time I combine working as a teacher with advancing my studies in education, and developing literary material for use by High School students."

DAWN FRENCH (St Lucia)
1964- She is a student of architecture and began writing poems and short stories in high school. "My style varies according to the subject of the poem; this is something I feel is as important as the subject matter." She has published poetry in newspapers in St. Lucia and in *New Voices* in Trinidad and Tobago.

JOAN FRENCH (Jamaica)
1945- She has been active in the women's movement in Jamaica since 1969 and is known for her work in the Sistren Theatre Collective. She is a founding member of CAFRA and has been co-ordinator of CAFRA's "Women in Caribbean Agriculture" project since 1988. She is co-author (with Honor Ford-Smith) of a pioneering historical study, *Women, Work and Organisation in Jamaica, 1900-1944*, and has produced the popular publications *No to Sexual Violence* and *Wid Dis Ring*. "Where does poetry fit in? In moments of quietness, to soothe my soul, crystallise my thoughts, and wrap me in the sense of wholeness between emotion, spirit and thought."

CORNELIA FRETTLÖH (Germany/Barbados)
1955- She is a free-lance writer who has lived in Barbados since 1983. She is a volunteer in the regional peace movement and a communications consultant to Women and Development Unit (WAND). Her poetry has been published in newsletters and magazines including *BIM* in Barbados.

MARY GARCIA CASTRO (Brazil)
1941- "Today I teach in the University of Bahia, I develop research on women in the labour force, I write poems, and I am engaged in the solidarity movement against the imperialist intervention in Central America and in movements for democracy in Brazil. As a woman, I am in many struggles." Her publications include "Mary's and Eve's Social Reproduction in the Big Apple" in *Columbian Voices*, New York University, 1982.

LYDIA GEERMAN *(Curaçao)*

1949- She is a social worker and was raised in Aruba. She writes of herself, "Poetry provides me with a kind of inner strength. Actually I only write poetry when things get real tough." She does voluntary work in the Pro Breastfeeding organization in Curaçao. Her work has been published in *Chimichimi* (1981), and *Bosero* (1980/81).

CHARMAINE GILL *(Barbados/Britain)*

1965- She works as a public relations officer. She writes of herself, "I was bitten by the writing bug when I first got published at eight years of age. Since then I've flirted with the sciences (I started to study Medicine) but have now been 're-infected' and am searching for my true voice." Her poetry has been published in *First Encounter*, New Brunswick, Canada.

MARGARET D. GILL *(Barbados)*

1953- She works as Regional Adviser at UNIFEM. She writes of herself, "I grew up in a family of ten, with very few opportunities for social or economic advancement but with a mother who wrote poems for children to 'recite' at Sunday school, and with a father who saw to it that the whole family attended church. Acknowledgement of those early imparted tenets of education, creative expression and attention to the spirit helped to create those opportunities which led to my present life." Her poetry has been published in *BIM*.

LORNA GOODISON *(Jamaica)*

1947- She is a writer, "primarily a poet and a sometime short story writer." She was trained as an artist-painter and does the covers of her books. Her collection *I am Becoming My Mother* won the Commonwealth Poetry Prize, Americas Region. Her other publications include *Tamarind Season, Heartease* and *Baby Mother and the King of Swords*.

CAROLLE GRANT *(St. Vincent and the Grenadines/ Barbados)*

She has spent most of her writing life "in the advertising world writing copy for all media (West Indies and U.S.A.)." She is the mother of two sons and is devoted to 92 potted plants.

GLADYS AUGUST HALL (Belize)

1935- She is a Methodist teacher, church organist and mother. She writes of herself, "I enjoy being with people. I feel I can identify with the less fortunate. Varied situations sometimes give me much food for thought and it is during these moments that I am prompted or inspired to put my thoughts in writing: hence my poems, songs and short stories." Her poetry is published in *Belizean Poets, Vol. 3*.

CLAIRE HARRIS (Trinidad and Tobago/Canada)

She came to Canada from Trinidad and Tobago in 1966 and settled in Calgary, Alberta, where she teaches English in the Separate Schools. In 1975 she began to write for publication. Her books include *Fables from the Women's Quarters* (1984) for which she won a Commonwealth Prize, *Travelling to Find a Remedy* (1986) for which she won the Alberta Culture Poetry Prize, and the Writer's Guild of Alberta Poetry Prize. Her latest work is *The Conception of Winter* (1989).

GINA HENRIQUEZ (Aruba)

1938- She is the President of a Modern Secondary School Foundation. She writes of herself, "At the age of 14 I began to write poems. At that time I wrote a poem in English and ever since I always use the English language to write and express myself. At times I also write in Papiamento (our native tongue)." She writes poems, short stories, and stories for children.

GERMAINE Y. HORTON (Trinidad and Tobago)

1948- She works as a secretary and writes poetry. She has read poems (not her own) on radio. Her publications include "Christmas Poems for Children" in *Peoples Magazine*.

AUDREY INGRAM-ROBERTS (Jamaica/Bahamas)

1951- She works as a management and training consultant. She has been writing poetry for over 15 years and has been greatly influenced by the Jamaican poet, Christine Craig. "I would like to believe that my poetry is about the tapestry of relationships and experiences that influence my cosmology."

CELENE JACK (St. Vincent and the Grenadines)
She is a social worker and an active church lay worker. She writes of herself, "My extensive work in Co-operatives and among women and youth, brings me face to face with the sharp realities of life in under-developed societies...and gives me a keen understanding of the needs of women...and establishes solidarity with the suffering masses of women internationally, in particular, our down-trodden but strong sisters in South Africa."

JANET JAGAN (U.S.A./Guyana)
1920- She is a journalist and political activist. She is a founding member of the People's Progressive Party (P.P.P.)(1950). She was Deputy Speaker of the House in 1953 and held ministerial positions in Guyana 1957-1964. She is President of both the Women's Progressive Organisation (W.P.O.) and the Union of Guyanese Journalists. Her publications include *Army Intervention in 1973, Elections in Guyana,* and *History of the P.P.P.*

MERYL JAMES-BRYAN (Trinidad and Tobago)
1948- She works as a consultant in culture and communications, and writes articles, poetry and fiction. She has recently completed her first full-length work of fiction. Her work has been published in *Essence, Black Enterprise, BWIA Sunjet Magazine,* and the *Trinidad Express.*

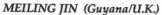

MEILING JIN (Guyana/U.K.)
1956 - She was born in Guyana and went to England in 1964. She is a black belt in karate and enjoys T'ai Chi. She visited China in 1981 and was deeply moved by the experience. She has written several children's stories and some of her writing has appeared in the *Funky Black Women's Journal.* Her first published collection of poetry is called *Gifts from my Grandmother.*

AMRYL JOHNSON (Trinidad and Tobago/U.K.)
She is a poet and writer and lives and works in England. She has worked extensively in the British school system, mainly as a writer-in-residence. Her publications include *Shackles, Sequins for a Ragged Hem,* and *Long Road to Nowhere.* Her work has been included in *Facing the Sea,* and *Watchers and Seekers,* among others.

STACY JOHNSON (Trinidad and Tobago)
1971- She is a high-school student. She writes of herself, "I have always loved reading and writing poetry. I am ecstatic that the women of the Caribbean have been given this chance to express themselves."

LORRAINE F. JOSEPH (U.S. Virgin Islands)
1927- She is a retired teacher and administrator and was elected to the Virgin Islands Academy of Arts and Letters in 1973. She writes of herself, "I engage in writing poems, short stories and plays, and am working with a small independent publishing company to produce Caribbean materials. I enjoy doing poetry readings and storytelling for elementary schools." Her publications include *My Island*, a children's book.

LEONIE KESSELL (Australia/St. Lucia)
1931- She has worked as an advertising writer in London. She has lived for many years in Trinidad and Tobago and in St. Lucia, where she teaches Sociology. She has deep interests in sailing and racing, and lives on a yacht.

C. CARRILHO-FAZAL ALI KHAN (Suriname)
1943- She works as a librarian. Her publications include "Het bibliotheekwezen van het Cultureel Centrum Suriname" in *Deskundigen aan het woord*, Sticusa, 1971.

BELEN KOCK-MARCHENA (Aruba)
1942- She is a teacher who has maintained a consistent interest in poetry. She also does painting and sculpture. She writes, "My first published poem was 'Puffrouw ik heb een botter meegebrengt'. In this poem I wanted to express my feelings for our children, who get lessons in a language that is not theirs." She also writes in Papiamento.

RANDI GRAY KRISTENSEN (Jamaica/U.S.A.)

1960- She is a writer, radio producer and cultural activist. She lived abroad for many years and returned to Jamaica to recapture "language, colour, rhythm." She is a founding member of Creative Harmony Club, an organization of rural Portland women. She has also written and produced radio programmes on Caribbean women writers.

RUFFINA LEE SHENG TIN (Trinidad and Tobago)

1958- She has been a teacher of Transcendental Meditation (T.M.) since 1978 and helps run the International Meditation Society of Trinidad and Tobago. She writes, "My mother has had a particularly strong influence on my own desire for strength and independence as a woman while at the same time maintaining some of the softer feminine values."

SHARON LEE WAH (Trinidad and Tobago)

1961- She graduated from the University of the West Indies (U.W.I.) in 1982. She writes, "I started studying law in 1982. In November 1982 I was seriously hurt in an automobile accident and since then I have been slowly recovering." Her poetry has been published in *Gayap*.

AUDRE LORDE (U.S. Virgin Islands)

Black woman, poet, essayist, lesbian, feminist, mother, activist, daughter of Grenadian immigrants and cancer survivor, her poetry has appeared in numerous periodicals and anthologies both in the United States and abroad, and has been translated into many languages. She is the author of 13 books and lives in St. Croix, U.S. Virgin Islands.

JOY MAHABIR (Trinidad and Tobago)

1966- She is a student and a writer. She writes of herself, "I have now committed myself to writing and think this is the only way to live." At present, she lives and studies in New York. Her work has been published in the *Naparima Girl's High School Magazine*.

NIALA MAHARAJ *(Trinidad and Tobago)*

1952- She lists her occupation as a "displaced journalist." She writes of herself, "I have worked as a teacher, journalist and librarian and currently am unsatisfactorily roving the world, working in development NGOs and hoping. I would really like to settle down and write prose because poetry is only an involuntary unbidden excuse for existence at present."

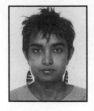

AHDRI ZHINA MANDIELA *(Jamaica/Canada)*

She is a Toronto-based theatre artist and performance dub poet. She concentrates much of her literary and stage work in the public school system. She is a political activist and works, as well, through poetry and community organs such as Black MERES (a Black mother's anti-racism collective). Her publications include *Speshal Rikwes*.

MARINA AMA OMOWALE MAXWELL *(Trinidad and Tobago)*

1934- She is a writer, lecturer and video producer. She founded the Yard Theatre in Jamaica in the 1960s and the Writer's Union in Trinidad and Tobago in 1980. She has worked in the media in London, Jamaica and Trinidad and Tobago. Her publications include *The Weakened Sex, About Our Own Business, and Chopstix in Mauby*.

PAULINE MELVILLE *(Guyana/U.K.)*

1948- She is an actress and works mainly in English theatre, television and film. She has also worked briefly in Jamaica. She writes of herself, "Born of a Guyanese father and English mother, I maintain strong links with family and friends in the Caribbean." She is now working on a collection of short stories.

NANCY MOREJÓN *(Cuba)*

1944- She is a writer whose poetry has been translated into various languages and has appeared widely in anthologies. She has also translated poetry by Jacques Roumain and Aime Cesaire. Her critical works include *Lengua de Pajaro (Bird's Tongue)* 1971, and *Nacion y mestizaje en Nicolas Guillen (Nation and Racial Mixture in Nicolas Guillen)*. Her published works include *Mutismos (Silences)* 1962, *Amor, Ciudad Atribuida (Love, Attributed City)* 1964, and *Cuaderno de Granada (Grenada Notebook)* 1984.

356

AMY NICHOLAS *(Belize)*
1949- She is a primary school teacher in Corozal, Belize. She is married and the mother of four children.

GRACE NICHOLS *(Guyana/U.K.)*
1950- She is a writer and has also worked as a journalist. She went to Britain in 1977. Her first collection of poems, I is a long memoried Woman, won the 1983 Commonwealth Poetry Prize. Her other books include *The Fat Black Woman's Poems* and a novel set in Guyana, *Whole of a Morning Sky.* She has also written several books for children.

NORMA NICHOLS *(Guyana)*
1934- She is a teacher and writes of herself, "My teaching career spans twenty-five years of arduous work." She has worked, furthered her education continuously and raised seven children. "Since childhood I had been writing poetry but it was not until 1977 that I printed my first book." Her publications include *Thoughts are Things, Thoughts have Wings* and *Potpourri with a Taste of Cult.*

GRACE NOBBEE-ECCLES *(Trinidad and Tobago)*
1910-1988. She was a teacher and wrote consistently throughout her life. Her published works include *For Small Fry* (1957), and *English With Tears* (1940).

SITA PARSAN *(Suriname)*
1945- She has worked as a typist, and as a teacher of Surinamese migrants in Holland, including 6 months of work in a detention centre. She writes, "My poems are couriers. They give impulses and courage to lift up Suriname from the downward position into which we pushed her." Her work has been published in newspapers in Suriname and in a periodical in Guadeloupe.

NAN PEACOCKE *(Guyana/Canada)*

She was born in the year of the Rat, and lives in the Caribbean, wherever she is — between the devil and the deep blue sea. Her work has been published in *Fireweed* and in the *Women's Studies Journal*, Canada. She was, for many years, the editor of *Woman Speak*, a publication of WAND, out of Barbados.

NORA E. PEACOCKE *(St. Vincent and The Grenadines)*

1912- She worked as the editor of *The Vincentian* newspaper between 1973 and 1989. She has also worked in the Agricultural Department in St. Vincent and the Grenadines, the Caribbean Commission in Trinidad and Tobago and the Scientific Research Council in Jamaica. She has written numerous editorials and has been published in newspapers throughout the Caribbean.

JOYCE PETERS-MCKENZIE *(St. Vincent and The Grenadines)*

1939- She is a writer and has also worked as a high-school teacher and an administrator. She writes of herself, "I began creative writing in November 1985 and am currently engaged in it full-time." Her work has been published in *New Voices*, and *Pathways*. She is working on a novel, *Man Born Ya*.

MARLENE NOURBESE PHILIP *(Tobago/Canada)*

1947- She is a writer, poet, university lecturer and lawyer who lives in Toronto. She is the winner of the 1988 Casa de las Americas literary prize for poetry. Her poetry and prose have been extensively anthologized. She has published three books of poetry, *Thorns, Salmon Courage,* and *As She Tries Her Tongue Her Silence Softly Breaks* and one novel, *Harriet's Daughter*.

VELMA POLLARD *(Jamaica)*

1937- She is a Senior lecturer in Language Education at the University of the West Indies. She writes poetry and short stories. Her publications include three anthologies for schools, one collection of short stories and one of poetry.

PHYLLIS PUNNETT *(St Vincent and The Grenadines)*
1917- She is a retired high school teacher. She wrote the words of the National anthem of St Vincent and the Grenadines. Her poetry has been published in the newspaper in St Vincent and the Grenadines.

ASHA RADJKOEMAR *(Suriname)*
1965- She is a writer and a student of literature. She also devotes time to Indian dancing. Her work has been published in *Bhasa* (Suriname) and *Deus Ex Machina*, Belgium.

VANDA RADZIK *(Guyana)*
She is a writer, poet, and a lecturer in English at the University of Guyana. She has been active in the women's movement in Guyana and the Caribbean.

JENNIFER RAHIM *(Trinidad and Tobago)*
1963- She is "a student of West Indian literature and so far a part-time creative writer. In 1981 I had my first public exposure in the pages of the New Voices. I attempt to form my saying through poetry and fiction." She has published in the *New Voices*, and the *Trinidad and Tobago Review*.

TRIVENI RAHIM *(pseud.) (Trinidad and Tobago)*
1957- She is a feminist activist and is also a graduate student. She writes of herself, "I am a Caribbean woman of Indian ancestry — my father was on the last ship load of labourers to come to Trinidad under the Indentureship system. My intellectual and socio-cultural life has been spent grappling with issues of class, race and gender."

RAJANDAYE RAMKISSOON-CHEN *(Trinidad and Tobago)*

1931- She works as a consultant obstetrician and gynaecologist. She started writing poetry in 1985. Her poems have been published in newspapers in Trinidad and Tobago and in the *Trinidad and Tobago Review*.

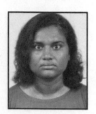

INDRANI RAMPERSAD *(Trinidad and Tobago)*

1952- She is a research student and the editor of *Jagriti*. She has spent some time studying in India. She writes, "I am particularly interested in raising the consciousness of Indian women in Trinidad and Tobago and improving their national image. I am also interested in working with grassroots women of diverse ethnic and racial groups."

GIANNINA ELENA RIJSDIJK *(Suriname)*

1954- She works as a curriculum developer for adult education. She has also been a teacher. She writes, "I started writing in 1969 encouraged by a revival in Surinamese literature during the late sixties and the early seventies. My advice to poetesses: Listen to your children and write. What comes out of their mouths is pure poetry." She has had short stories published in *Viva*, (Holland).

DAWN MAHALIA RILEY *(Trinidad and Tobago)*

1970- She has been writing since the age of eleven. She writes of herself, "My main goal in life is to continue writing and to publish a volume of work by the age of 25." Her poems have been published in *New Voices* (Trinidad and Tobago), and in the local newspapers.

NELCIA ROBINSON *(St. Vincent and the Grenadines)*

1947- She is a community educator and active feminist. She is the coordinator of the Committee for the Development of Women (C.D.W.) in St. Vincent and the Grenadines. She writes of herself, "I am a woman in politics and contested the 1984 and 1988/9 General Elections in St. Vincent and the Grenadines." Her publications include *Poetry is Feeling, Pictures Remain* and *Melée*.

TIFFANY ROBINSON (Trinidad and Tobago)
1970- She is a high school student who has written several poems. Her work has been published in *The House*, a school magazine.

LEONE ROSS (U.K./Jamaica)
1969- She is a student and writer. She was editor of her high school magazine and has written several articles for the *Women's Feature Service*. She writes of herself, "I came to JA with my mother at the age of six. I have been greatly affected by West Indian situations (politics, male/female relationships) and started writing poetry at about ten years old."

RUMEENA (pseud.) (Suriname)
1960- She works in the telecommunications industry as an organizational analyst. She has been writing poetry since 1980.

EVELYN ST. HILL (Guyana)
1937- She works as a caterer. She writes of herself, "I live with my twin sister and an elderly family friend in an old-fashioned cottage in the heart of Georgetown... I love to walk, write, bake, play scrabble and also to visit older housebound friends."

ELAINE SAVORY (U.K./Barbados)
1948- She is a university lecturer and writer. She writes of herself, "I am at this point in my life settled in the Caribbean, from which experience the poetry comes. I am involved in theatre and also write prose and academic material." Her poetry has been published in journals in the U.S.A. and the Caribbean.

RUTH SAWH *(Trinidad and Tobago/U.S.A.)*

She is a writer and a university lecturer. She writes of herself, "I have two sons who keep me busy. Their vocabulary is limited at times to "Cook, cook, cook"...I think that many other women can accomplish their goals or close to them if only they dare to start with what little they have." Her publications include *Rotiless Ramgoolie*.

SEKETI *(Suriname)*

1960- She is a self-defined "African-Surinamese Black Feminist." She is trained in Political Economics and is now a student of Women and Development Studies in Amsterdam. She writes, "I like to write feminist poetry in my leisure time. I read all prose and essays that I can get written by black women, also their poems. I have an ardent correspondence with black and white women about issues like racism, sexual politics, social problems of black women living in Europe and those living in the so-called 'Third World'."

OLIVE SENIOR *(Jamaica)*

She has worked as editor of *Jamaica Journal* and *Social and Economic Studies*. Her collection of short stories, *Summer Lightning*, won the first Commonwealth Writers Prize in 1987. Her other publications include *A-Z of Jamaican Heritage, The Message is Change, Talking of Trees* and *The Arrival of the Snake Woman*.

KIREN SHOMAN *(Belize/U.K.)*

1972- She is a highschool student. She writes of herself, "I wrote the poem 'They Liked Me Then' at 15 years of age. I am interested in studying literature and enjoy writing poetry.

HAZEL SIMMONS-MACDONALD *(St. Lucia/U.S.A.)*

1947- She is a teacher and a writer. She is currently working in children's literature. She prefers the medium of prose but also writes poetry. Her poetry has been published in *Savacou*, and *Toutwelle*.

DOROTHY WONG LOI SING (Suriname)
1954- She works in the field of adult education. She writes of herself, "I love to write, to read Caribbean, Surinamese and Third World Literature. I love to paint in oils and black ink; I love jazz and calypsoes." Her publications include "Zwarte Muze" and "Sudan Man, I'd rather cut your throat than allow your people to circumcise me."

DEBORAH SINGH-RAMLOCHAN (Trinidad and Tobago)
1958- She is a teacher of English. She began writing at high school in the Creative Writing Club. She is currently working on her first collection of poetry.

SHIRLEY SMALL (Trinidad and Tobago/Canada)
1936- She is a teacher and a writer. She is also the co-editor of Kola (Montreal) and the Vice President of the Montreal chapter of the Congress of Black Women of Canada. Her work has been published in *Kola, Simone de Beauvoir Instititute Newsletter*, and *Graffiti*.

RUTHEEN TAYLOR (U.S.A./Belize)
1920- She is now a farmer and a writer. She was involved in the education of retarded children for many years and established her own school. She has written numerous articles on children's theatre, creative expression and education. Her publications include *Poetic License* (Florida, U.S.A.)

LELETI TAMU (Jamaica/Canada)
She is a shelter worker and a counsellor. Her nationality is AFRICAN! She is a dyke, mother, poet, doing the left thing in a right-minded society. Her work has been published in *Our Lives, Dykewords* and in *Fireweed*.

YVONE MECHTELLI TJIN-A-SIE (Suriname)

1935- She is a writer whose first work was published in 1973. She is stimulated by travel and has been to countries in the Caribbean, North American and Europe. She has published 3 books of poetry and 8 of prose fiction. Her publications include *Akoeba* (1973), *Broko den Skotoe* (1974), *Askete and Emilina*.

ANNETTE L. TROTMAN (Barbados)

1956- She works as a cultural officer in the field of Theatre Arts. She writes of herself, "I am basically involved in show business as a performer, producer, director and technical person. I am also a journalist and poet." She has published articles in the *Nation* newspaper and is known for features such as "Bajan Folkways," and "Caribbean Folkways."

IMELDA VALERIANUS-FERMINA (Curaçao)

1916- She is a writer and an actress. She recently played the role of an 'echado' di kuenta' (storyteller) in the film Almasita di Desolato, an internationally highly praised production from Curaçao. Her collections include *Eamor di Juansito, Aventura di Lucas Winterhorti, Mi Pensamenta* (1985), and *Komanikashon* (1988).

TONI VUURBOOM (Trinidad and Tobago)

1924- She works as a manufacturer's representative and runs a small business. She began writing poetry at age five and loves writing satirical poems and calypsoes. She has also composed several Parang (Spanish carols) songs. Her publications include *The Fields are White*.

GLADYS WATERBERG (Suriname)

1959- She is a community development worker and a poet. She writes of herself, "I became aware of the socio-economic situation of my country and committed myself to doing something about it by joining in the revolutionary process which was born in February 1980... My poems are a reflection of my feelings, love for my country and especially the socio-economic position of women." Her publications include *Aspasja (Purbe Considere), Xora* (on posters), and the poem "In Bro."

MARGARET WATTS *(Trinidad and Tobago/U.S.A.)*
She is a university lecturer and poet. She has lived and taught in India, Ghana, the U.K., the U.S.A. and Trinidad and Tobago. Her publications include *White and Black Ivory*. Her work has also been published in numerous journals.

MARIE-ELLA WILLIAMS *(Trinidad and Tobago)*
1955- She is a writer and artist and works as a copywriter for radio. She writes of herself, "I see myself as a writer/artist with a deep interest in what is indigenous. I'm involved, at present, in hand-colouring fabrics and researching various aspects of folk culture."

JOY WILSON-TUCKER *(Bermuda)*
1942- She is the editor of the *Manchester Bulletin*, Bermuda and has been writing for the last twenty years. She was the provincial Grandmaster of the Mayflower Lodge in Bermuda. Her publications include *Bermuda, Isle of My Heritage* (1983), and *Images of Bermuda* (1984).

MARGUERITE WYKE *(Canada/Trinidad and Tobago)*
1927- Her main interests are art, literature and music. She was a senator in the now defunct Legislature of the Federation of the West Indies. Her poems have been read over the B.B.C. and published in *BIM, Voices, New World* and *Canadian Forum*.

Up to the publication deadline the following contributors' biographies were not available:

V.M ALBERT *(St. Lucia)*
FROME CULTURAL CLUB *(Jamaica)*
JANE KING HIPPOLYTE *(Barbados)*
ANGELIQUE MARSAN *(Suriname)*
NNEKA *(St. Vincent and the Grenadines)*
MARTHA TJOE-NIJ *(Suriname)*

GLOSSARY

abeng	a cow's horn or conch shell used as a musical instrument and for signalling, especially among the Maroons, who had a code of signals which was never divulged to any but their own people. It is still used today in Westmoreland as a summons.
a-bwile	aboil, boiling
All skin teet nuh larf	all smiles are not genuine laughter.
ajoupa	thatched hut
anansi	a spider, legendary trickster figure of Afro-Caribbean folk-tales, with West African roots
awndah	under
babbilan, babylon	Rastafarian term for the world of non-believers
back-dam	canefields in Guyana, usually separated by wide canals
backra	a white person
bans o'	a lot of
bickle	cooked food
Black Bottom	an area in downtown Toronto where the population is mainly black
blood-cloth	sanitary towel
bly	break, ease, as in "gimme a break"
bullpistle	the dried penis of a bull, used as a weapon
Bun Pan	a thrift society for the low income earner
bush-tea	herbal infusions of many varieties, prescribed for different ailments
buss-up-shot	paratha roti, which is a variety of bread made by Indians with a texture resembling torn clothing
calypso	a musical and lyrical comment on any subject, usually composed for, but not limited to, the Carnival season
cane trash	waste left after cane is harvested
carat	carat palm, used mainly in Trinidad and Guyana in rural areas to make thatched roofs for peasant dwellings
carn-fish	corned-fish: preserved by salting

367

Carnival	Carne vale. Farewell to the flesh in preparation for the Lenten season. The festival itself starts with J'Ouvert (daybreak) on Monday morning and ends at Las' Lap on the Shrove Tuesday night before Ash Wednesday
compere	male companion or friend
chulhah	a clay fireplace used for cooking by Indians in Trinidad and Guyana
degge, degge	only, sole, single
dem seh wen hag nuh grow dem call am pig	They say when a hog does not grow up, they call it a pig
deputy	mistress, also the other woman or (rarely) man in a love triangle
diablesse, la diablesse	in folk legend, a beautiful lady of the night, who seduces male passers-by. She has one cloven foot, usually hidden under her long skirt.
douen	in folk legend, the souls of unbaptised children who live in the forest. They are neuter in gender and their feet are pointed backwards.
dred, dread	Rastafarian. The name refers to the dreadlocks (long, uncut hair) usually worn by followers of this religion and way of life.
dungle	ghetto
duppy	ghost
dutty tuff	the ground is hard
Englington	England
fahrin	foreign
farine	cassava flour
flag woman	one who dances and waves the flag in front of a steelband or a band of masqueraders
flambeaux	a light source made of a cloth wick and a kerosene-filled bottle
forceripe	ripened by force and still immature
Garifuna	Black Caribs who live in Belize, Central America
haffi	have to
heddication	education
hi-brong	high-brown, a reference to a light complexion
Hoo nuh hear guh feel	Who will not listen must feel

hougan	voodoo priest
I and I, I 'n I	Rastafarian speech, referring to the usual "I" first person, nominative case
indentureship	refers to the system of indentureship, which replaced slavery in the Caribbean. Under this system, labourers, mainly Indians, were brought to the West Indies for work on the sugar-cane plantations. The greatest concentrations were in Trinidad and Guyana.
inna, eena	in
Jah	Jehovah, Rastafarian term for God
jamette	a prostitute
J'ouvert morning	opening of the day...a time when revellers take to the streets in rags and old clothing, usually satirizing current issues, to mark the opening of Carnival
Kekchi	a group of Maya Indians who live in the Central part of Belize, Central America
kersene ile	kerosene oil, used for domestic fuel
keys	a version of "cays", it refers in this case to the tiny islets off the coast of St. Vincent and the Grenadines
kiskeedee	large, yellow-breasted bird with a characteristic call which sounds like "Qu'est qu'il dit?"
kyan	cannot
lick, licks	a beating
like yarm fit Joshua mout	like yam fits Joshua's mouth; the height of appropriateness
locksed	wearing hair in Rastafarian fashion
logie	barrack-type structure which offered cramped housing to slaves and indentured labourers in the West Indies
mac'mere, macumere	a good female friend
ma deveen	ma divine, an honorific given to an older woman of authority and respect in the community
manicou	rodent-like marsupial, eaten as a delicacy
mawga, mahgah, maaga	lean, thin, scraggy
miggle	middle

movay-lang	mauvais langue, to ill-speak or gossip about someone
never-see-come-see	a person who has recently been exposed to unaccustomed circumstances of good fortune, wealth or an elevated social position, and who displays tasteless ostentation as a result
nyam	to eat, especially roughly or voraciously
nutten	nothing
ole' mas	revellers dressed in rags, old clothing and makeshift costumes on J'ouvert morning
ongle	only
Orisa mother, (also Orisha)	a female leader of the Shango religion in Trinidad and Tobago
Oya	a female deity in the Shango religion in Trinidad and Tobago. She is the mistress of the wind and the rain.
Pania	Spaniard
Papa Bois	in folk legend, father of the woods and its surroundings, half man and half beast, with cloven feet
possie	posse
poui	large flowering tree with brilliant yellow blooms, blossoms in April and heralds the coming of rain
punta	a popular dance in Belize, with folk roots
Rastafari	a member of a cult which originated in Jamaica, and which takes Ras Tafari as its name-patron, and holds that the Emperor of Ethiopia is God incarnate
skin up	laugh with
sinting	something
Sisserou	a species of parrot (Amazona Imperialis) found only in Dominica, one of the world's endangered species
smaddy, smady	somebody
soucouyant	in folk legend, a female vampire, who sheds her skin at night, and transforms herself into a flying ball of fire
speshal rikwes	special request
queeze	squeeze

seh	say
shingle	shilling
shurance	assurance
tassa	drum made of stretched goat-skin, traditionally played at Indian festivals and ceremonies in Trinidad and Guyana
tenor pan	a type of steelpan
The Harder They Come	a film, set in Jamaica about the life of a singer trying to make it through the jungle of the music industry there
wabine, guabine	a prostitute, literally a fresh-water sardine, very common to streams and canals
Waitukubuli	Carib name for Dominica
wata-rate	water-rate
wining, wine, winds	to rotate the waist and hips in a suggestive manner while dancing
yabba	heavy earthenware bowl of any size, (small bowls up to large cooking pots) commonly used in households
y'eye	eye
Youlou	Carib name for St. Vincent

The following sources have been consulted in the compiling of this glossary:

1. Bennett, Louise. *Jamaica Labrish*, Jamaica: Sangster's Book Stores, 1966.

2. Cassidy, F.G. & Le Page, *R.B. Dictionary of Jamaican English*, London: Cambridge University Press, 1980.

3. Hall, Robert A. *Haitian Creole*, New York: Kraus Reprint Co., 1969.

4. Honychurch, Lennox. *The Dominica Story: a history of the island.* Dominica: 1975.

5. Mendes, John. *Cote ce cote la: Trinidad and Tobago Dictionary*, Trinidad & Tobago, 1985.

6. Simpson, George Eaton. *The Shango Cult in Trinidad*, Puerto Rico: Institute of Caribbean Studies, 1965.